Ursula
k. Le Guin

RECOGNITIONS

detective/suspense

Raymond Chandler By Jerry Speir
P. D. James By Norma Siebenheller
Ross Macdonald By Jerry Speir
Dorothy L. Sayers By Dawson Gaillard
Sons of Sam Spade: The Private Eye Novel in the '70s
By David Geherin

science fiction

Ray Bradbury By Wayne L. Johnson
Critical Encounters: Writers and Themes in Science Fiction
Dick Riley, Editor
Frank Herbert By Timothy O'Reilly
Ursula K. Le Guin By Barbara J. Bucknall
Theodore Sturgeon By Lucy Menger

Also of Interest

The Bedside, Bathtub & Armchair Companion to Agatha Christie
Dick Riley and Pam McAllister, Editors
Introduction by Julian Symons

Ursula k. Le Guin

Barbara j. Bucknall

Frederick Ungar Publishing Co. New York

Copyright © 1981 by Frederick Ungar Publishing Co., Inc.

Printed in the United States of America

Design by Marsha Picker

Library of Congress Cataloging in Publication Data

Bucknall, Barbara J.
  Ursula K. Le Guin.

  (Recognitions)
  Bibliography: p.
  Includes index.
  1. Le Guin, Ursula K., 1929–   —Criticism
and interpretation. I. Title. II. Series.
PS3562.E42Z58   813′.54   81-10371
ISBN 0-8044-2085-8   AACR2
ISBN 0-8044-6063-9 (pbk.)

Second Printing, 1982

For copyright acknowledgments and credits,
see pages 159-160 and following.

This book is dedicated to my parents,
in the hope that they will enjoy it.

Contents

Foreword

The work of Ursula K. Le Guin is very dear to me, as I have never lost my childhood love of the marvelous. For a long time now I have been reading science fiction and fantasy, in English, as a change from the "serious work" of studying French literature. This habit reached its peak in 1955, when I read the first two volumes of *The Lord of the Rings* by J. R. R. Tolkien while preparing for my Oxford B.A. final examinations in modern languages. As a result, I found myself preoccupied with Middle Earth when my mind should have been on French and German. I might have obtained a better degree had I not been immersed in Tolkien, but I shall never forget the rapture with which I read him.

After reading other writers of fantasy and science fiction, about ten years ago I discovered Le Guin. Le Guin's *A Wizard of Earthsea*. Le Guin seemed to me to strike the same note as Tolkien, although her works are shorter and slighter. Since then I have been reading everything by her that I can find—purely for pleasure. I had no idea of writing a book about her until this was suggested to me by the editors of Frederick Ungar Publishing Co.

Once I began to work on this book, I found myself involved in studying many aspects of Le Guin's work that I had previously ignored. The publication of *The Language of the Night*, a collection of her essays on fantasy and science fiction, came as a welcome help. Le Guin's criticism of her own work is a model for her critics. As I went on, my enthusiasm for her writing was sharpened by research. I hope to have conveyed something of that enthusiasm in my book, which is devoted mainly to Le Guin's fantasy and science fiction. Although her Orsinian stories are excellent, they are not true fantasy and so have been mentioned only briefly.

The structure of this book is fairly simple. The introduction, "A Look at Le Guin" consists of a summary of Le Guin's life and achievement. After that, her works are described in roughly chronological order, with particular emphasis on her novels and novellas. For an exact account of the order in which Le Guin's works were published, the reader should refer to the chronology as well as to the bibliography.

The notes indicate the sources of all quotations in the text (except those from the works being discussed). All quotations are identified by page number and the last three words of the quotation. References to works by critics, without quotation, are identified by the critic's name.

As I worked on this book, I received much help from Ursula K. Le Guin herself. To her I owe heartfelt thanks for her many kind and thoughtful answers to my letters. I should also thank James Allen, an associate of her literary agent, Virginia Kidd, who has provided useful information. And Dick Riley, my editor, deserves thanks for the help I have received from him. I would also like to offer a word of appreciation to several friends and relations who have discussed my work with me, making helpful suggestions and providing useful information and general encouragement. These are my cousin Margaret Macaulay, my brothers Malcolm and Bill Bucknall, my friends Richenda Kramer, David Beam, and Frank and Tom Alberti, and my student Bob

Powers. The Brock University reference librarian, Sylvia Osterbind, and the librarian of the Kristine Mann Library, Doris Albrecht, also assisted me. Of course, I appreciate the work of the many critics who have written on Le Guin. And I wish to thank Virginia Arthur and Inés González-G. de Oro, without whose typing this book could not have been completed in time.

B. J. B.

Chronology

1929 Ursula Kroeber is born on October 21, in Berkeley, California, to Alfred L. Kroeber and Theodora K. Kroeber.

1947 Enters Radcliffe College, Cambridge, Massachusetts.

1951 She is a member of Phi Beta Kappa and receives a B.A. from Radcliffe. She enters Columbia University.

1952 Receives an M.A. from Columbia University and begins work on a Ph.D.

1953 Having received a Fulbright fellowship, she leaves for France and meets Charles A. Le Guin. They marry in Paris.

1954 Instructor in French at Mercer University, Macon, Georgia.

1956 Instructor in French at the University of Idaho.

1957 Daughter Elisabeth is born.

1959 Daughter Caroline is born. The Le Guins settle in Portland, Oregon.

1960 Alfred L. Kroeber dies.

1962 Le Guin's first fantasy story, "April in Paris," is published.

1963 Her first real science-fiction story, "The Masters," is published.

1964 Son Theodore is born.

1966 Le Guin's first science-fiction novel, *Rocannon's World*, is published. *Planet of Exile* is also published.

1967 *City of Illusions* is published. Parnassus Press asks her to write a book for older children.

1968 Works for Eugene McCarthy in the Oregon primary.

Theodora K. Kroeber marries John Quinn. Le Guin accompanies her husband and children on a sabbatical trip to England. *A Wizard of Earthsea* is published.

1969 *The Left Hand of Darkness* is published and wins a Nebula Award. Le Guin gets the *Boston Globe-Hornbook* Award for Excellence in Text for *A Wizard of Earthsea*.

1970 Receives a Hugo Award for *The Left Hand of Darkness*.

1971 Teaching participant in a writers' workshop at Pacific University and is writer-in-residence at the Clarion West (science fiction) workshop at the University of Washington. *The Tombs of Atuan* and *The Lathe of Heaven* are published.

1972 Le Guin wins a Newbery Honor Book Citation for *The Tombs of Atuan*. She works for George McGovern in the Oregon primary and continues as writer-in-residence at the Clarion West workshop at the University of Washington. "The Word for World Is Forest" and *The Farthest Shore* are published.

1973 Writer-in-residence at the Clarion West workshop at the University of Washington. She is given the National Book Award for Children's Literature for *The Farthest Shore* and a Hugo Award for "The Word for World Is Forest."

1974 Teaching participant in a workshop on writing science fiction at Portland State University. *The Dispossessed* is published and wins Nebula and Jupiter Awards. Le Guin is also awarded a Hugo for "The Ones Who Walk Away from Omelas" and a Nebula for "The Day Before the Revolution."

1975 Le Guin wins a Hugo Award for *The Dispossessed*. Teaching participant in a workshop on writing science fiction at Portland State University, writer-in-residence at a science-fiction workshop held near Melbourne, Australia, and guest of honor at "Aussiecon," a world conference of science-fiction fans held in Melbourne. "The New Atlantis," *Wild Angels*, and *The Wind's Twelve Quarters* are published.

1976 Visiting Fellow in Creative Writing at the University of Reading in England. *Very Far Away from Anywhere Else* and *Orsinian Tales* are published.

1977 *Nebula Award Stories Eleven*, a collection of award-winning science-fiction stories by various authors, edited by Le Guin for the Science Fiction Writers of America, is published. She is a teaching participant in a workshop on writing science fiction at Portland State University. "The Diary of the Rose" receives a Jupiter Award.

1978 *The Eye of the Heron* is published, and Le Guin participates in the Indiana University Writers Conference.

1979 Theodora Kroeber-Quinn dies. Le Guin wins the Gandalf Award presented by the 1979 "Worldcon" for achievement in fantasy. Teaching participant in a workshop on writing science fiction at Portland State University. A collection of her critical writing is published as *The Language of the Night: Essays on Fantasy and Science Fiction*, edited by Susan Wood. *Leese Webster* and *Malafrena* are published.

1980 *The Lathe of Heaven* is shown on television. *The Beginning Place* is published, as is *Interfaces*, a collection of science-fiction stories by other authors edited by Le Guin with her literary agent, Virginia Kidd.

1

A Look at Le Guin

This popular author, whose works express warm feelings and strong moral values as well as a vivid imagination, was born in Berkeley, California, on October 21, 1929. She was named after St. Ursula, whose day it was; but this has not left her with any aspirations to sainthood. Le Guin's values are human ones.

Le Guin was very fortunate in her family; if she had chosen her parents herself, she could hardly have done better. Her father, Alfred L. Kroeber, was the eminent anthropologist; her mother, Theodora K. Kroeber, was herself later to become a writer. Being people who thought deeply and read widely, they encouraged the full development of their children's minds. Such intellectual liveliness combined well with Ursula's own imagination and depth of feeling.

With three brothers—Theodore, Clifton, and Carl—Le Guin was the youngest member of her family. The two eldest were the sons by her mother's previous marriage. Theodora had lost her first husband through an early death, just as Alfred had lost his first wife. There is no indication, however, that the Kroeber children were anything but happy and united; their father treated them all excellently.

Much can be learned about him from Theodora Kroe-

ber's book, *Alfred Kroeber: A Personal Configuration* (1970). He
appears to have been a truly good man, kind and affectionate,
simple in his ways, with an original turn of mind and
remarkable abilities. It is clear what a loss his death, in 1960,
was to his family. His wife has little to say about herself, but
in *Again, Dangerous Visions*, Vol. I (1972), Harlan Ellison says
that, on seeing her, one could easily understand where Le
Guin had "obtained her elegance and style." The extremely
high level of personal behavior and personal relationships
that marks Le Guin's writings and sets them apart from so
much modern writing can reasonably be traced to her
experiences with her family.

During the university year, the Kroebers lived in Berkeley, where Alfred L. Kroeber taught. But during the sum-
mers they had the good fortune to retreat to Kishamish,
their summer residence in the Napa Valley. It had everything
to make it a children's paradise. Forty acres spread around
a redwood house and barn, an expanse well explored by the
children with the help of Juan Dolores, a Papago Indian.
Probably much of Le Guin's delight in describing journeys
on foot stems from these early explorations of what must
have seemed unlimited territory.

Many visitors came to Kishamish, ranging from writers
and scholars to graduate students, Indians, and relatives.
From this background Le Guin picked up an awareness of
anthropology. Two of the basic principles that she absorbed
were an awareness of the variety of the human family and
a respect for the very different ways of life that human
beings can adopt. These principles make it impossible for
the anthropologist to indulge in false superiority, intolerance,
or bigotry when faced by a human group, no matter how
strange. Le Guin's books are, in consequence, full of vastly
diverse modes of existence that are, nevertheless, recognizably human.

Alfred L. Kroeber is chiefly known for his work on the
California Indians, although he wrote voluminously on many
topics; and his feeling toward those Indians was one of

friendship and respect, a friendship and respect shared by his wife. One can see this particularly well in Theodora K. Kroeber's book *Ishi in Two Worlds* (1961), which is rightly well known. Some people think that the Kroeber children must have known Ishi, the last wild Indian left alive in North America, because he was such a friend of their father. In fact, Ishi died in 1916. But they certainly imbibed the attitudes that made it possible for the professor and the Indian to be friends.

Le Guin tells how her father used to narrate Indian legends. But the Kroeber children were nourished not only on Indian tales and legends. Le Guin read a great deal of myths, legends, and fairy tales during her childhood. The Norse myths were especially dear to her and shaped her imagination. At the age of twelve she opened Lord Dunsany's *A Dreamer's Tales* (1910), which she found on the living room bookshelves, and was amazed by the very first paragraph. It described the "Inner Lands" of Toldees, Mondath, and Arizim, bounded to the east by a desert, to the south by magic, to the west by a mountain, and to the north by the Polar wind. In "A Citizen of Mondath" (1973), an essay that explains her involvement in science fiction and fantasy, she says that Dunsany came to her as a revelation. This was in spite of her familiarity with legends and myths. She continues:

> What I hadn't realized, I guess, is that people were still making up myths. One made up stories oneself, of course; but here was a grownup doing it, for grownups, without a single apology to common sense, without an explanation, just dropping us straight into the Inner Lands. Whatever the reason, the moment was decisive. I had discovered my native country.

This revelation occurred at a time when Le Guin was already writing fantasy herself. She still has her first completed short story, written at the age of nine, about a man who was persecuted by evil elves. But the fact that Dunsany was an adult writing for adults put the question of writing

fantasy in an entirely new perspective. Dunsany was to her
a liberator and guide, although she has never attempted to
imitate him.

Another childhood influence on her development was
her discovery of the writings of the Chinese philosopher Lao
Tse, also known as Lao Tsu and Lao Tzu,* who is a more-
or-less legendary figure. Tradition has it that he was born
in 604 B.C., which would make him a contemporary of
Confucius, whom he is supposed to have corrected on a
number of occasions. But, if he ever existed, he may have
been born later. He is known for the collection of precepts
attributed to him, called the *Tao Te Ching*. "Tao" is a Chinese
concept that has to do with acting instinctively in the right
way on all occasions and in all difficulties. It is normally
translated as "the Way." Arthur Waley's translation of the
Tao Te Ching bears the title *The Way and Its Power*, which
suggests the mysterious but strongly ethical nature of this
work. There are many translations of the *Tao Te Ching*. They
are all markedly different, owing to the obscurity of the
original Chinese.

The *Tao Te Ching* is one of the fundamental texts of
Taoism, which teaches an attitude of noninterference and
of refusal to be involved in the Confucian world of states-
manship, bureaucratic control, and observance of rites. In
her essay, "Dreams Must Explain Themselves" (1973), in
which she discusses the creation of her Earthsea trilogy, Le
Guin says that her attitude toward literary creation is linked
to her interest in Taoism. In her creative work she feels that
she is discovering places and people rather than inventing
them. In the same way, she sees Taoism as implying discovery
of the way things work. In this connection, she says:

> The Taoist world is orderly, not chaotic, but its order is not
> one imposed by man or by a personal or humane deity. The
> true laws—ethical and aesthetic—are not imposed from above

* Throughout this text, the form Lao Tse—and later, Chuang Tse—is
being used. This is in line with Le Guin's preference.

by any authority, but exist in things and are to be found—discovered.

In addition to her early interest in fantasy and Taoist philosophy, Le Guin was also familiar with science fiction. In the early forties, she and her brothers read a great deal of science fiction in *Thrilling Wonder* and *Astounding*. She says that they looked for trash because they liked trash. It amused them. When she was ten or eleven she wrote her first science-fiction story and submitted it to *Amazing Stories*. It was rejected, but this did not cause her particular distress. In any case, her interest in science fiction waned before too long:

> I never read only science fiction, as some kids do. I read everything I could get my hands on, which was limitless; there was a house full of books, and a good public library. I got off science fiction some time in the late forties. It seemed to be all about hardware and soldiers. Besides, I was busy with Tolstoy and things. I did not read any science fiction at all for about fifteen years, just about that period which people now call The Golden Age of Science Fiction. I almost totally missed Heinlein, et al. If I glanced at a magazine, it still seemed to be all about starship captains in black with lean rugged faces and a lot of fancy artillery.

The summary phrase, "Tolstoy and things," does not tell us a great deal about Le Guin's preferences in literature. But it seems that she developed a taste for the great literature of many countries and times, with a preference for the novels and poetry of the nineteenth century. The Romantics appealed to her romantic temperament, and she admired the solid craftmanship of such authors as Tolstoy and Dickens. She appreciates careful attention to plot and characterization, and one sees this in the list of "influences" she drew up in 1976:

> My own list of "influences" might go Shelley, Keats, Wordsworth, Leopardi, Hugo, Rilke, Thomas and Roethke in poetry.

Dickens, Tolstoy, Turgenyev, Chekhov, Pasternak, the Brontës, Woolf, E. M. Forster in prose. Among contemporaries, Solzhenitsyn, Böll, Wilson, Drabble, Calvino, Dick.

It is worth noting that the Thomas she mentions is Edward, not Dylan. It is also interesting that only two of the novelists she mentions, Calvino and Dick, have any connection with fantasy and science fiction.

Italo Calvino, an Italian, writes mainly fantasy, in a lighthearted and highly intelligent vein, delighting in puzzles and paradoxes. One of his most fascinating works, *Il castello dei destini incrociati* (1969), translated as *The Castle of Crossed Destinies* (1977), is based on the symbolism of the Tarot, a special deck of twenty-two cards used for fortune-telling. Philip K. Dick, whom Le Guin admires so much that she has written an article, "The Modest One" (1976), to protest the general public's failure to appreciate his works at their true value, is a very prolific American science-fiction writer who specializes in portraying "ordinary" people with extraordinary gifts and in extraordinary situations. Le Guin obviously came to Calvino and Dick much later than to many of the other authors she mentions. She probably read many of the earlier writers when she was still quite young. Certainly she would have read Victor Hugo and Leopardi in the course of her formal education.

When she went to college in 1947, Le Guin studied French and Italian, specializing in Renaissance literature. She obtained her B.A. from Radcliffe College in 1951 and her M.A. from Columbia University in 1952. Her studies were distinguished, and she became a member of Phi Beta Kappa. She started work on a doctoral program, preparing a thesis on the poet Jean Lemaire de Belges, but gave it up when, in December 1953, she married Charles A. Le Guin, whom she had met while on her way to a Fulbright year in France. She and her husband, who is a professor of French history, have three children: Elisabeth, born in 1957, Caroline, born in 1959, and Theodore, born in 1964. They live in Portland, Oregon. One can suppose that Le Guin values her marriage because she gives a great deal of importance to marriage in her writings.

Her preference is for a quiet, regular life. She has said:

> I like it kind of dull basically. I like a very regular life. Life is pretty complicated; three kids and writing, Charles teaching and so on. We have to be fairly regular in our hours or we wouldn't get it all done.

Her amusements are quiet ones. When she is not reading or writing, she likes to spend time with her family. She also likes to look at pictures and listen to music. Her favorite painter is Turner and her favorite composers, who figure in some of her short stories, are Beethoven and Schubert. As far as outside involvements are concerned, she did some teaching before her children were born and then again when they were older. She took part in nonviolent peace demonstrations in the sixties and worked for Eugene McCarthy and George McGovern in their primaries. But one feels that her favorite activity which she has never interrupted for long— is writing.

Le Guin's marriage put an end to her doctoral dissertation but not to her true work. On the contrary, her marriage gave her the opportunity to continue writing. She wrote numerous poems, which are collected in *Wild Angels* (1975). In the space of ten years, starting in 1951, she wrote five novels. Four of them were about Orsinia, an imaginary country in central Europe, and one was set in San Francisco. The novels about Orsinia were not science fiction or fantasy, but neither were they realistic. They were rejected by several publishers who said that they seemed remote. Le Guin says that they were intended to be remote, that she had hit upon a way of "distancing" her material from the reader, so that there was room for the imagination. But the real trouble was that her books did not fit into any known category, which made it impossible to publish them in America unless she had a name. Since the only way she could get a name was by publishing, she had to find a category into which she could fit.

Although she read and admired J. R. R. Tolkien's *The Lord of the Rings* when it first came out in the 1950s, she did not attempt to imitate him. A far more direct influence on her is traceable to 1961, when a friend in Portland lent her a copy of *Fantasy and Science Fiction* that contained "Alpha Ralpha Boulevard" (1961) by Cordwainer Smith (the pseudonym of Paul Linebarger). In this story, Smith retells the story of *Paul et Virginie* (1788), a tale by the early Romantic writer Bernardin de Saint-Pierre about two young lovers on the island of Mauritius, whose love is destroyed when Virginie perishes in a storm. Smith's retelling is a highly sophisticated blend of literary allusion and his own brand of science fiction. Le Guin does not really remember what she thought when she read it, but she started looking for more of that kind of thing.

As a result of her renewed interest in science fiction, she decided to try to fit her writing into the category of fantasy and science fiction. Since she did not know much science, the stories she wrote were "fairy tales decked out in space suits"—which helped to sell them but did not make them genuine science fiction. Her stories were published in the early sixties by Cele Goldsmith Lalli, the editor of *Amazing* and *Fantastic*. Little by little, Le Guin taught herself more science and began to get accustomed to her medium. Her first science-fiction novels were *Rocannon's World* (1966), *Planet of Exile* (1966), and *City of Illusions* (1967). They show an interest in anthropology and even in extrasensory perception rather than in technology, and have a distinctly romantic, magical tone. Le Guin says of these early works:

> The first science fiction story I wrote that begins to break from the trivial became the source, and prologue, of the little novel *Rocannon's World*. I was beginning to get the feel of the medium. In the next books I kept on pushing at my own limitations and at the limits of science fiction. That is what the practice of an

art is, you keep looking for the outside edge. When you find it you make a whole, solid, real, and beautiful thing; anything less is incomplete. These books were certainly incomplete, especially *City of Illusions*, which I should not have published as it stands. It has some good bits, but is only half thought out. I was getting vain and hasty.

Le Guin's first truly successful work—and probably her greatest achievement—is the Earthsea trilogy: *A Wizard of Earthsea* (1968), *The Tombs of Atuan* (1971), and *The Farthest Shore* (1972). *A Wizard of Earthsea* won the *Boston Globe-Hornbook* Award for Excellence, *The Tombs of Atuan* won a Newbery Honor Book Citation, and *The Farthest Shore* won the National Book Award for Children's Literature. This tale of the life and adventures of a wizard is straight fantasy and does not suffer in any way from comparison with *The Lord of the Rings*.

The Left Hand of Darkness (1969), Le Guin's first science-fiction novel that did not contain elements of fantasy, won both the Hugo and Nebula Awards. (The Hugo Award is presented by science-fiction fans and the Nebula Award by science-fiction writers.) This novel takes place during an ice age on the planet Gethen, which is peopled by androgynes. The very ancient symbol of the androgyne is used here to show what it means simply to be human, once one has disposed of sex roles. This is Le Guin's first contribution to feminism, which she has always taken seriously but without being particularly militant.

The Lathe of Heaven (1971) investigates dream states and satirizes the power complex of some psychiatrists, particularly behaviorists. *The Word for World Is Forest* (1972), which won a Hugo Award and which first appeared in *Again, Dangerous Visions*, Volume I, a collection of science-fiction stories on problematical topics edited by Harlan Ellison, also considers dream states but is primarily a satire on American involvement in Vietnam.

The Dispossessed (1974) won Hugo, Nebula, and Jupiter Awards, the latter of which is presented by instructors of science fiction in higher education. This novel, which reflects the author's increased understanding of physics, presents anarchism in a sympathetic light. Le Guin finds anarchism the most interesting kind of political theory. To her, anarchism implies opposition to authoritarian government and a conviction that people are basically willing to help one another. She does not incline to the stereotyped view of the anarchist as a terrorist who wants to bring about chaos. Her anarchism is closely linked to her Taoism in its taste for an organic order rather than an imposed one. Her horror of a repressive, authoritarian government is apparent in "The New Atlantis" (1975).

As interest in Le Guin has grown, many of her short stories have been reprinted in *The Wind's Twelve Quarters* (1975). Two of the pieces in this collection have won awards. "The Ones Who Walk Away from Omelas" (1973) won a Hugo, and "The Day Before the Revolution" (1974) won a Nebula. The stories in *The Wind's Twelve Quarters* are a mixture of fantasy and science fiction, and some are quite surrealistic.

Not published in *The Wind's Twelve Quarters* were four very imaginative and, for the most part, very funny short stories that were still in print in various anthologies when *The Wind's Twelve Quarters* was issued. Eight more short stories on science-fiction and fantasy themes have appeared between 1976 and 1980. Of these, "The Diary of the Rose" (1976), which combines political protest with a loving description of the qualities of two sensitive and creative minds—all in the context of science fiction—won a Jupiter Award.

Other publications have been *Orsinian Tales* (1976), a collection of short stories about her imaginary country; *Very Far Away from Anywhere Else* (1976), a short novel without any fantasy elements that depicts the love of two sensitive and talented young Americans; and *The Eye of the Heron*, published in *Millennial Women*, edited by Virginia Kidd (1978), a short novel that portrays the difficulties involved in being a pacifist in a violent society. This latter work, like *The Word for World is Forest*, reflects Le Guin's involvement in the peace movement. Finally, the four most recent works to appear are *The Language of the Night* (1979), a collection of her essays and talks on science fiction and fantasy; *Leese Webster* (1979), a children's story about a creative spider; *Malafrena* (1979), a novel about Orsinia set in the early nineteenth century; and *The Beginning Place* (1980), a mixture of realism and fantasy of a kind that she had previously used only in much shorter works.

Le Guin has also edited two anthologies of other people's work: *Nebula Award Stories Eleven* (1977) and *Interfaces* (1980). The latter volume, edited jointly with Virginia Kidd, her literary agent, reflects Le Guin's preference for sensitive work with a strong emphasis on human feeling and a minimal use of technology.

Her enthusiasm for science fiction is such that Le Guin likes to encourage others to write it too, and it seems that she has success in teaching it. Le Guin is a member of Science Fiction Writers of America and has conducted workshops in science-fiction writing in the United States and in Australia. The Australian session is described, with examples of the work produced, in *Ursula K. Le Guin's Science Fiction Writing Workshop: The Altered I*, edited by Lee Harding (1976). After giving this workshop, she was guest of honor at "Aussiecon," the world conference of science-fiction fans held in Melbourne, Australia, in 1975. She has also given courses in the writing of science fiction and fantasy at universities in the United States and England.

She very much enjoys getting together in workshops with other writers to create science fiction. In her introduction to *Ursula K. Le Guin's Science Fiction Writing Workshop: The Altered I*, she says that she finds participating in the group that forms at any one of these workshops very exciting and invigorating. It is a welcome change from working alone and makes her think of what working together must be for musicians—not competition but emulation. In a workshop there is a coming together of talents and skills for mutual support and improvement. Such cooperation is a realization in aesthetic experience of the anarchist ideal of mutual aid that Le Guin presents in *The Dispossessed*. It is also far more creative than ordinary classroom teaching, where the teacher and students seldom emulate each other and where imagination can be conspicuously absent.

Fantasy and science fiction appeal to Le Guin because of their use of the imagination. She says:

> People keep predicting that I will bolt science fiction and fling myself madly into the Mainstream. I don't know why. The limits, and the great spaces of fantasy and science fiction are precisely what my imagination needs. Outer space, and the Inner Lands, are still, and always will be, my country.

But, as she says in "Science Fiction and Mrs. Brown" (1977), the writer of science fiction and fantasy should also be a portrayer of character. She admires the work of Dick, Lem, and the English writer D. G. Compton because they present real human beings at grips with difficulties that, however bizarre they may be, call forth all the protagonists' human resources. She herself has done her best to see her protagonists in terms of character, and this, together with her use of metaphor, is what makes her stories and novels come alive. In this connection, she writes:

> Unless physical action reflects psychic action, unless the deeds express the person, I get very bored with adventure stories; often it seems that the more action there is, the less happens. Obviously my interest is in what goes on inside. Inner space. and all that.

Le Guin's emphasis on soundness of character and accuracy of psychological presentation also helps to give her writings their strong ethical tone. We feel that she is describing real people, so what they do really matters. Her seriousness also adds to this feeling. She has written some very funny short stories, such as "Intracom" and "Schrödinger's Cat" (both 1974), but as a general rule, although the characters in her novels laugh at times, the jokes they laugh at are quite mild. Laughter in the works of Le Guin expresses affection and companionship more often than a keen sense of the ridiculous.

She is also an outstanding stylist. She expresses herself clearly, vividly, and poetically while resisting the temptation to overwrite. Her style, which varies from book to book and from character to character, does not have the stately and heroic tone of *The Lord of the Rings*. And yet what she says of Tolkien's style, as opposed to the "Poughkeepsie" (or fake fantasy) style, is to a certain extent true of the way she writes herself.

> Clarity and simplicity are permanent virtues in a narrative. Nothing highfalutin' is needed. A plain language is the noblest of all.
>
> It is also the most difficult.
>
> Tolkien writes a plain, clear English. Its outstanding virtue is its flexibility, its variety. It ranges easily from the commonplace to the stately, and can slide into metrical poetry, as in the Tom Bombadil episode, without the careless reader's even noticing. Tolkien's vocabulary is not striking; he has no ichor; everything is direct, concrete and simple.

This tribute to Tolkien is a statement of the standard Le Guin sets for herself.

Because Le Guin succeeds at meeting her own high standards, it is hardly surprising that she has received so much recognition. The awards she has won are many, the latest being the Gandalf Award presented at the 1979 Worldcon—World Conference of Science Fiction Fans—for achievement in fantasy. But even with their high standards, neither Tolkien nor Le Guin would have won popularity if they had not been really good storytellers with interesting tales to tell. There is a hunger in today's world for the marvels and adventures that are markedly absent from mainstream fiction. Le Guin satisfies that need while maintaining an excellence for which her fans are grateful. It is a real pleasure to examine the ways in which she arrives at that excellence and to see her ability grow from her early novels to her mature work.

2

The Hainish Cycle Begins

T he early science-fiction novels of Ursula K. Le Guin are not as good as her best novels, but they have a great deal of charm, particularly for those who like a mixture of science fiction and fantasy. This combination is especially effective in *Rocannon's World* (1966), of which Le Guin says:

There is a lot of promiscuous mixing going on in *Rocannon's World*. We have NAFAL and FTL spaceships, we also have Brisingamen's necklace, windsteeds and some imbecilic angels. We have an extremely useful garment called an impermasuit, resistant to "foreign elements, extreme temperatures, radioactivity, shocks and blows of moderate velocity and weight such as swordstrokes or bullets," and inside which the wearer would die of suffocation within five minutes. The impermasuit is a good example of where fantasy and science fiction *don't* shade gracefully into one another. A symbol from collective fantasy—the Cloak of Protection (invisibility, etc.)—is decked out with some pseudoscientific verbiage and a bit of vivid description and passed off as a marvel of future technology. This can be done triumphantly if the symbol goes deep enough (Wells's Time Machine), but if it's merely decorative or convenient, it's cheating. It degrades both symbol and science; it confuses possibility with probability and ends up with neither.

Le Guin is hard on herself. In the light of her later achievements, she has every right to be. And if she had not been hard on herself, if she had not continually demanded more of herself, if she had not been prepared to take science fiction and fantasy with the utmost seriousness, treating her medium with full respect for its potential, the achievements of the Earthsea trilogy, *The Left Hand of Darkness,* and *The Dispossessed* would never have been attained.

Rocannon's World stems from a short story written in 1963 and published as "Dowry of the Angyar" in 1964. Also titled "Semley's Necklace" in *The Wind's Twelve Quarters* this tale serves as the prologue to the novel *Rocannon's World.* The central character is Semley, a woman so tall and beautiful that she looks like a goddess. In fact, she *is* a goddess, for Le Guin based her story on that of Freya, the Norse goddess, and her Brisingamen necklace, as retold in Padraic Colum's *Children of Odin* (1920). As Le Guin says in her 1977 introduction of *Rocannon's World,* she read *The Children of Odin,* and later the Eddas, many times and was deliberately borrowing from Norse myth in this novel.

According to Padraic Colum's version, the goddess Freya wanted to go to three giant women who lived on a mountain top and made beautiful things out of gold. But she did not speak of this desire to her husband Odur, for she knew he would disapprove. Instead, she left her home in secret, leaving Odur with their little daughter Hnossa. She went down to the earth and asked the elves the way to the mountain. But they would not tell her. The dwarfs, however, agreed to tell her if she would spend the night in their caves with them. They spent the night kissing her, greatly to her distaste, and then showed her the way to the mountain. The three giant women gave her a golden necklace called Brisingamen, and she was happy to have it. But when she returned to Asgard, she found that Odur, in his displeasure at what she had done, had left her. She sought him for a long time, but never found him. Her only comfort was Hnossa, who had grown during Freya's search into a beautiful young goddess.

Le Guin has made few changes to this story. Semley, the wife of a poor but noble lord on Fomalhaut II, longs for a gold and sapphire necklace that once belonged to her family, which would permit her to outshine other women as her husband outshines other men. She is advised against this, but leaves her castle, without her husband's knowledge, to search for it. She goes to the Fiia, who are small humans, clearly based on elves, and they tell her it may be found among the Clayfolk, who are equally clearly based on dwarfs and who live under the ground. Against the advice of the Fiia, she goes to the Clayfolk, whose dwarfish skill has been adapted to constructing electric light bulbs and a subway, and they take her in a spaceship to another planet, where the necklace she seeks is kept in a museum. In the spaceship, the Clayfolk touch Semley until she resists their impertinence. Then in the museum she is seen by an ethnologist, Rocannon, who is sorry that her race had not been chosen for development by the League of All Worlds instead of that of the Clayfolk. He gives her the necklace and she returns home, only to find that, although she herself has not aged, sixteen years have passed in her journey through space. Her husband is dead and her daughter a young woman. In despair, she gives the necklace to her daughter and runs off into the forest, never to be seen again.

The story continues with Rocannon on her world, in the company of Semley's grandson, Mogien. Rocannon is not much older than he was when he saw Semley, for time passes slowly in journeys between the worlds. He has come to Fomalhaut II to conduct an ethnological survey. But rebels from the planet Faraday blow up the ship in which other members of his team were waiting for him, and Rocannon sets out with Mogien, some of Mogien's serfs, and a Fiian to track down the rebels at their base and send a message to his own planet, using their ansible, to warn the League of All Worlds of the rebellion.

This is the first of many references to the ansible, the marvelous radio that transmits news across space instantaneously. It will reappear in *City of Illusions, The Word for World*

Is Forest, and finally in *The Dispossessed,* where the hero, Shevek, discovers its governing principles. But in this early novel, Le Guin is not interested in exploring the scientific implications of this device.

For transport, the Angyar, the race of lords in this feudal society, use huge winged cats, called windsteeds. (Probably the idea of the winged cat came from Freya's chariot, which was drawn by two cats.) Le Guin has a lot of fun with the cattish nature of the windsteeds, describing with a cat-lover's affection their various cries. It is typical of her technique for inventing the creatures of different worlds that her windsteeds should be so much like enormous cats. Le Guin has no real interest in inventing bizarre fauna and flora. Just as her aliens are almost always recognizably human, even when they differ in some way from the human norm, so are her animals and plants almost always recognizably based on those we know on Earth. The Winged Ones and the Kiemhrir, whom Rocannon will meet on his journey, are based respectively on various hive-building insects and small furry creatures that abound on Earth. Le Guin does not even invent her own myths here, as she would do in the Earthsea trilogy and *The Left Hand of Darkness,* but sticks closely to old Norse mythology.

A lot of what happens to Rocannon and his escort fits quite easily into the Old Norse context. The Angyar even have dragon ships. And now that Semley is off the scene, Rocannon, the middle-aged ethnologist, takes on features of Odin. The Fiian calls him the Wanderer, which is one of the many names of Odin (and Padraic Colum's preference). A serf in a village they pass through refers to Rocannon as a *pedan,* which appears to mean a god.

As Rocannon and his companions make their way south toward the base of the Faradayan rebels, engaging in some heroic hand-to-hand fighting as they go, Rocannon is separated from the others and taken prisoner by a group of Olgyior (serfs) who are living without a lord. The leader of the serfs tries unsuccessfully to behead the captive. Then

Rocannon is tied to a hearth-post and a fire is lit around him. His clothes burn off and Semley's necklace, which Mogien's mother had given him, is revealed; but Rocannon is quite unharmed because he is wearing his impermasuit. Everyone who sees this is terribly frightened, but they keep him bound to the post. During the second night, Yahan, one of Mogien's serfs who had disobeyed his master and run away, comes and gives him water and loosens his chains. The next morning, Rocannon defies his tormentor and walks out, carrying a stick that is assumed to be a wizard's staff. Yahan finds him again, and the two meet up with Mogien and the others, after a further adventure in which Rocannon gives Semley's necklace away to save Yahan's life, only to have it returned by Mogien.

The previously narrated episode is based on a story, retold by Padraic Colum, of how Odin came to the hall of a king, Geirrod, whom he had brought up but who had become the leader of a band of robbers. To test him, Odin requested hospitality and was badly treated. Told to sing, Odin sang a song reproaching Geirrod, and as punishment was tied to one of the pillars of the hall with a fire lit under him. Odin was quite unharmed by the fire, but the cruel king kept him bound for nine nights. The servants were forbidden to bring him food or drink, but Geirrod's gentle brother, Agnar, brought Odin a horn of ale every morning at dawn. On the ninth night, Odin denounced Geirrod, freed himself from his chains and turned Geirrod and his followers into wild beasts.

A second Odin-inspired adventure takes place after Rocannon has rescued his companions from the Winged Ones, creatures that live in beautiful cities and look like angels but have minds like insects. (Occasionally, Le Guin gets so annoyed by Christianity that she cannot keep from getting in a dig at it, and this may be one of those occasions.) Rocannon's companions have been captured for the larvae of the Winged Ones to suck dry. They are helped to escape by some charming little creatures called the Kiemhrir, who can speak Mogien's language. Then, Rocannon, Mogien, and Yahan (the only survivors from the group that began the journey) cross a range of mountains.

High up in the mountains, Rocannon finds a cave with a stream running below it. In this cave lives a very ancient being who belongs to the race to which the Clayfolk and the Fiia belonged before they went their separate ways. This being has the power to unlock the gift of telepathy (or as Le Guin prefers to call it, mindspeech), and Rocannon learns how to listen in on the minds of the Faradayans. This corresponds to the gift of wisdom that Odin obtained by drinking at Mimir's well, for which he had to give up his right eye. Rocannon has to give up something very dear to him, too. This turns out to be Mogien, who single-handedly attacks a helicopter that is approaching them, and dies.

The story ends when Rocannon has used his gift of receptive telepathy to find the Faradayan base and sends the message on their ansible. The Faradayans are destroyed by a faster-than-light bomber. Rocannon survives long enough to marry a beautiful Angyar lady and give her Semley's necklace, and the world he has visited is named after him. So ends the first of Le Guin's quest tales. Its structure is episodic, taking the reader rapidly from one adventure to the next. Throughout, references to Semley's necklace link events and prevent the adventures from seeming too disconnected.

The second novel, *Planet of Exile*, is much more tightly plotted. On another distant planet, a group of Terran colonists, sent by the League of All Worlds six hundred Earth-years previously, gets news that a race of northern nomads, the Gaal, is moving south to escape the immensely long winter. Each season lasts fifteen years on this planet, and only a man who lives to be old, such as Wold, the chief of the Tevarans, the local native people, can live to see a second winter. The Tevarans, who have spent a nomadic summer on their ranges and are building their winter city, are not very impressed when Jakob Agat, a leader of the colonists, comes to warn them of the coming of the Gaal. They know that the Gaal come south every winter, and they are sure that they can defy them from within the shelter of their winter city. But this time, Jakob Agat tells them, *all* the Gaal, united under one leader, are migrating and attacking winter cities as they approach, in order to carve out an empire for themselves.

Wold, who is less affected than his compatriots by the traditional distrust and hostility between the colonists and the natives, agrees to send the Tevaran warriors, who will meet up with the colonists at an agreed point, to attack the Gaal as they move south and turn them aside. But before Wold can carry out this plan, his daughter Rolery, his child by the youngest of his wives, consents to a love affair with Jakob Agat. Some of her kinsmen attack Agat for this. Rolery finds him lying in the snow and takes him to the colonists' city. There she marries him. But a rift has opened between the colonists and the Tevarans and, for the moment, they cannot act together.

The Gaal arrive, destroy the Tevarans' winter city, and kill most of the men. Jakob Agat and Umaksuman, a son of Wold who is on the side of the colonists, lead a raid into the winter city and rescue a number of Tevarans, including Wold. They take them to Landin, the city of the colonists. Jakob Agat sends young children and their mothers, under Wold's leadership, out to a fortress in the sea at the end of a causeway. Rolery and most of the older women stay behind to help defend Landin against the Gaal.

The fight is fierce and many are wounded. Rolery helps tend the wounded, and it is she who points out to the doctor that their wounds are infected. The doctor does not believe her at first and becomes extremely angry with her for presuming to teach him his business. It is a principle of medicine among the colonists that they cannot be harmed by the local bacteria, as their chemical structure is slightly but significantly different from the local norm. They cannot even digest the local food without enzymoid shots or pills, the doctor tells Rolery.

Then it occurs to him that, for some time now, the colonists have been finding it easier to digest without help, and he suddenly realizes that the colonists have apparently adapted to this planet. This would explain why their women have had so many miscarriages in recent years. The miscarriages would be due to incompatibility between the mother and a normalized fetus, and instead of marriages between the local inhabitants and the colonists being sterile, as they had been in the past, cross-fertilization could probably take place. This gives Rolery hope that she will be able to bear her husband a son.

Soon, the Gaal are driven off by the winter weather—they had left for their southern migration too late—and by the efforts of the inhabitants of Landin. The old chief Wold dies a natural death, and Rolery and Jakob Agat look forward to their life together through the long winter. The tension and danger of the greater part of the novel are resolved in a happy ending that is not only happy for the newly married pair but also for all the survivors, who can form a new race, sharing the cultural achievements of the colonists and the traditional wisdom of the native people. The colonists will no longer call the natives hilfs (for Highly Intelligent Life Forms) and the natives will no longer call the colonists witches, which they had done because of the colonists' mysterious skills. All are to be men and women together.

It is typical of Le Guin that she should show so much happiness arising from a marriage of true minds, since love, friendship, and marriage are constant themes of hers. The love between Jakob Agat and Rolery is literally a marriage of true minds, since they are able to speak to each other, mind to mind, in spite of the fact that Rolery has had no training in mindspeech.

In the very first chapter of the book, which is told from Rolery's point of view, Rolery wanders far out on the sands, as far as the fortress at the end of the causeway. Jakob Agat, who is up on the causeway, sees her out on the sands just as the tide is about to come in, faster than a man can run, and bespeaks her. (This is a term invented by Le Guin, which means that he speaks to her mentally.) She hears him, runs to him, and escapes the tide just in time.

Jakob Agat is annoyed with himself for using mindspeech on a hilf, as he fears that this demonstration of his uncanny ability will antagonize the Tevarans just when the colonists need their help. But Rolery, who is very strong by nature, keeps this strange event a secret and uses it, unconsciously, to build a rapport between herself and Jakob Agat. This enables her to find him lying hurt in the snow, after he has been attacked by her kinsmen, when his more sophisticated friends in Landin are aware simply that he is in need, but do not know where he is or how to help him. She is also able to bespeak him.

The story is told from shifting points of view. Sometimes we see events through the eyes of Rolery, sometimes through the eyes of Jakob Agat, and sometimes through the eyes of Wold. But it is significant that the story starts with Rolery. Le Guin has a very interesting comment on her:

> Rolery, a young and inexperienced woman of a rigidly traditional, male-supremacist culture, does not fight, or initiate sexual encounters, or become a leader of society, or assume any role which, in her culture or ours of 1964, could be labeled "male." She is, however, a rebel, both socially and sexually. Although her behavior is not aggressive, her desire for freedom drives her to break right out of her culture-mold: she changes herself entirely by allying herself with an alien self. She chooses the Other. This small personal rebellion, coming at a crucial time, initiates events which lead to the complete changing and remaking of two cultures and societies.

Le Guin then goes on to say that Taoism got to her sooner than modern feminism did, and that she sees Rolery as an example of the effectiveness of *wu wei*, "action through stillness," as opposed to the futility of aggression.

But if Rolery is memorable, so is her father Wold. The old chief, who keeps his wisdom and dignity in spite of the inroads of old age, is very touchingly depicted, although he is represented as the leader of a primitive people whom the colonists are inclined to despise. When Wold receives Jakob Agat in his tent in the winter city, he leans against a pitch-coated urine basket. In contrast, the colonists have houses with glass windows, central heating, and running water (and presumably indoor plumbing, although this is not mentioned). The Tevarans are capable of some form of pottery, for they have bowls for their food, but the colonists drink their *ti* from translucent porcelain. The Tevarans have not invented the wheel, but the colonists arrived in a spaceship, although they are no longer capable of making one. The leaders of the colonists hold a council in a civilized manner, but the men of the Tevarans discuss matters of importance at a stone pounding. Nonetheless, true to the lessons Le Guin learned from anthropologists in her youth, she shows the Tevaran, Wold, as at least Jakob Agat's equal; and there is no suggestion on her part that, in marrying Rolery, Jakob Agat is marrying beneath him, although the other colonists find this marriage hard to take.

The ways in which Le Guin shows differences of character and social context by little, telling touches mentioned almost casually mark an advance on *Rocannon's World*, where characterization, apart from a general evocation of the heroic mold, is minimal. However, the characterization in *Planet of Exile* is more social than individual and is related to differences of nature and mores. Tevarans' unwillingness to gaze into another human being's eyes and their tendency to react to any strong emotion with a brief rush of tears are contrasted with the colonists' more earthly characteristics. She has not yet reached, in *Planet of Exile*, the complexity of characterization that she is to achieve in *The Left Hand of Darkness* and *The Dispossessed*, but she is on her way.

Another element that we see further developed in *Planet of Exile* is the theme of telepathy or mindspeech. The kind of direct contact that mindspeech makes possible has gone beyond the mindhearing that Rocannon used to track down his enemy. In fact, such mindhearing has become forbidden by the laws of the League of All Worlds, although one of the colonists breaks the law to spy upon the Gaal. The idea of an ethical limit to an extraordinary ability is typical of Le Guin, who, throughout her writings, is very concerned with ethics. Already in this early work, mindspeech has become what it is to be in her later novels—symbolic of a true communion of minds and of a total truthfulness based on love. It has nothing to do with ESP as something that can be practiced in the real world. Le Guin comments that ESP is a metaphor in her books, "not an observation, nor a prediction."

Mindhearing and mindspeech come into play at the beginning of *City of Illusions*, where a strange man stumbles into a forest clearing near a house in the eastern part of what was once the United States of America. The inhabitants of the house take him in, and one particularly gifted girl listens to his mind but can find nothing but a jumble. He is kept and trained as if he were a little child, and when he becomes adult once more in his feelings and perceptions, he becomes the lover of the girl who first saw him, Parth.

They could have lived happily together in the forest clearing indefinitely, but then there would have been no story. So the master of the house, Zove, summons Falk (as they call the stranger) to him and encourages him to set out to the city of Es Toch, in the west. This is the stronghold of the Shing, who apparently are the ultimate enemy against whom the League of All Worlds was originally formed. The Shing have triumphed and prevented men from regaining their former high level of technological achievement. But Zove suspects that Falk is a visitor from another planet and that he represents some kind of hope for mankind. If he goes to the Shing and confronts them, this hope may be realized. Zove has no idea how this will happen, but it turns out that he is right. Le Guin blithely attributes to him the gift of prophecy, which, without more ado, settles the matter. So Falk sets off, leaving Parth to her grief.

Those who have read *Planet of Exile* have been given a pretty strong hint of Falk's true nature and origin by a description of his eyes. They are yellow, apart from the pupil, and have no visible white, like a cat's eyes. They are the eyes of Rolery, and the reader guesses that they are the eyes of a descendant of Rolery and Jakob Agat. There are other clues, as well. Falk shows the distress that Rolery felt on listening to human music. He also speaks of the slight difference that separates him from the human genetic norm. But it is not until the last part of the book, when Falk arrives at Es Toch and meets a compatriot, a boy who came with him in a spaceship from their world, that we know for certain who and what Falk is and why he came to Earth.

The boy, Har Orry, greets him as prech Ramarren, and tells him of the interbreeding of the Tevarans and colonists (or Alterrans, as he calls them). The new mixed culture flourished. Apparently the Tevarans were willing to learn from the Alterrans, and the Alterrans were no longer held back by the cultural inferiority of the Tevarans. The Law of Cultural Embargo, as Seiko Esmit explained to Rolery in *Planet of Exile*, prevented colonists from using many things that were different from those the native people used. But when the Tevarans came into close contact with the Alter-rans, they raised their cultural level sufficiently that the Alterrans were able to resort to their books and start using their old skills once more. Once the Tevarans started learning new ways, they were no longer an underdeveloped people who could be destroyed by sudden contact with an advanced civilization. Little by little the new, mixed race, the Kelshak nation, became capable of building spaceships. However, they did not rediscover the ansible, so when they wanted to find out what was happening on Earth, they had to go and look.

They had every reason to wonder what was happening, for they had received no news from Earth for over twelve hundred Earth-years. Shortly after their arrival, the colonists had learned that the enemy against whom the League of All Worlds had been formed had reached Earth. To bring help to Earth, the spaceship went back, taking with it the ansible and a third of the colonists. But it never returned to Werel, as the Tevarans' planet is called.

Har Orry thinks that the Shing are his friends and that they saved him when the spaceship on which the Kelshak emissaries were traveling was attacked by men. But Falk, who has been among men and heard their side of the story, knows better. He realizes that it was the Shing who attacked their ship when it entered planetary space and the passengers blacked out. It was the Shing who razed his mind and abandoned him in the forest, to live or die. His personality and memories as Ramarren have been erased. But in Es Toch the Shing tell him that they have not been erased permanently. They can erase the new, Falk mind and bring back Rammaren if he consents.

The Shing want to restore Falk's orginal mind because they want to know the location of Werel. Hal Orry, whom the Shing had assumed knew the information, did not; he was not sufficiently advanced when he left home to have learned the true name of his planet's sun. But the Shing think that Ramarren, who was the navigator of the Kelshak spaceship, can tell them. Falk realizes that the Shing's intentions for Werel are sinister and desparately attempts to retain his personality and memories as Falk after he submits to the operation that will restore his Ramarren identity.

He succeeds in this attempt and consequently has two minds. He uses this strange gift to gain control of a Shing who had overpowered the Ramarren side of his mind but was unaware that the Falk side lay in wait. Seizing his advantage, Falk-Ramarren gets the Shing to take Orry and himself to the spaceship that had been prepared for Orry, so that the boy could carry back to Werel the message that all is well on Earth. Turning the tables on the Shing, Falk-Ramarren kidnaps him, and the three set off for Werel. So ends another successful quest.

Zove's premonition that Falk represents a hope for mankind turns out to be correct, since the Kelshak nation has skills of mindguarding that enable them to cope with the Shing's mindlying. But neither Zove nor Parth will benefit from this; the journey to Werel takes about one hundred and thirty years, and Falk-Ramarren has not the time or the ability to fetch Parth when he sets out for Werel. For once, the hope represented by love seems to have failed. But instead of love—apart from a general love for mankind and Falk-Ramarren's specific responsibility for the boy Orry—it is truth that is the central theme in this tale.

The Shing are presented as the ultimate villains, successful liars, and the enemy that eighty worlds had learned to fear. But they are not convincing. Le Guin, who is her own best critic, says so herself:

> The modern cliché is: Bad people are interesting, good people are dull. This isn't true even if you accept the sentimental definition of evil upon which it's based; good people, like good cooking, good music, good carpentry, etc., whether judged ethically or aesthetically, tend to be more interesting, varied, complex and surprising than bad people, bad cooking, etc. The lovable rogue, the romantic criminal, the revolutionary Satan are essentially literary creations, not met with in daily life. They are embodiments of desire, types of the soul; thus their vitality is immense and lasting; but they are better suited to poetry and drama than to the novel. . . . Real villains are rare; and they never, I believe, occur in flocks. Herds of Bad Guys are the death of a novel. Whether they're labelled politically, racially, sexually, by creed, species, or whatever, they just don't work. The Shing are the least convincing lot of people I ever wrote.

What is it that the Shing actually do? They have mind-razed Ramarren and, presumably, all the other adult members of his expedition. That seems terrible when we first meet him stumbling through the forest. But the kindness he meets with in Zove's House is so effective in giving him a new mind that mindrazing loses some of its horror for us, and we become optimistic about his survival. Of course, the other members of the expedition from Werel presumably perished miserably, or else they were rescued and lived unobtrusively on the alien planet. Not much attention is given to them, so their plight does not really touch us.

There is a certain horror when Falk (as he then is) falls into the hands of the Shing and is subjected to a series of visions that appear to be at least partly drug induced. But this torture does not rise above a level of petty nastiness, something like the teasing of depraved children; and when Falk is finally allowed to meet the Shing face to face, their unnaturalness does not, at first, seem to exceed a taste for transvestism and heavily disguised foods. They also use drugs and have addicted Har Orry, but his dependence is to an apparently mild drug, because he is still able to function quite well. The sheer horror that Le Guin inspires, by a shadow whispering beside a door in *A Wizard of Earthsea,* or by the total ruin of the hazia eaters in *The Farthest Shore,* is missing here. If anything, the Shing seem rather pitiful, lost on a world that is not their own and yet ruling it, without any joy in their conquest.

Of all the characteristics of the Shing, the most absurd—the capability to think a lie—is the one that comes across as most sinister. Of their aptitude for lying, Le Guin says that she welcomed

> the chance to speak of civilization not as a negative force—restraint, constraint, repression, authority—but as an oppor-tuntiy lost, an ideal of Truth. The City as goal and dream. The interdependence of order and honesty. No work or moment or way of being is more or less "real" than any other, and all is "natural"; what varies is vividness and accuracy of perception,

clarity and honesty of speech. The measure of a civilization may be the individual's ability to speak the truth.

Lying is so deeply ingrained in the Shing that they do not even attempt to make their lies plausible, but lie for the sheer fun of it. In connection with their one law, reverence for life, Le Guin says that they have been fooled by their own lie. Again, even at their most sinister, the Shing are pitiable.

The Shing oppress their subjects and do not allow them to build cities or congregate in groups of more than two hundred. But the reader, if aware of the problems posed by modern cities, may not be sorry to see the cities go. Le Guin takes such obvious pleasure in describing an America returned to the wilderness that it cancels out her other intention, to show "the City as goal and dream." There is a kind of "small is beautiful" pleasure in following Falk across a continent as he encounters settlements set in mile upon mile of forest followed by prairie. Americans of today like to hark back to the times of the pioneers, before the wilderness was tamed; and it is easy to feel that if the Shing have brought back the wilderness, they cannot be so bad.

The vitality of the human beings Falk meets on the way to Es Toch does not seem to be entirely sapped by the Shing. Some of them, like the men who question Falk with a truth drug and throw him in their cellar, are terrified of the Shing and allow that fear to distort their lives. Others, like the members of the Basnasska Nation who live and hunt on the prairie, have reverted to savagery. Not even the tolerance of the anthropologist can make their attitudes and beliefs seem other than brutish. Nonetheless, we meet more individuals and groups who organize their lives with dignity and a sense of the fitness of things.

Besides Zove's House, there are other houses in the forest where people suffer from nothing more than a sense of isolation and the awareness that they cannot reach out too far. The old Listener, a natural empath, whom Falk meets in the forest, seems quite happy to live by himself. People disturb him, because he cannot avoid observing their emotions. He would be miserable in a city. Other independents include the tribe of the Bee-Keepers, who seem like medieval warrior-monks, impressive in their self-sufficiency and sense of purpose. The self-styled Prince of Kansas has great natural dignity and is born to command. He is completely at home in his little kingdom, and it would be difficult to imagine him in any city we know today. These people are all alive, alert, and self-reliant. Joy has not left these inhabitants of Earth, as it will for the inhabitants of Earthsea in *The Farthest Shore*.

One of the less pleasant characters in *City of Illusions* is Estrel. There is a passivity in her love-making that exasperates Falk. But although Falk is repeatedly warned against her, he trusts her and does not connect her passivity and apathy with the influence of the Shing. This affects our view of her. And although she is an instrument of the Shing and betrays Falk into their hands, she delivers him to his planned destination in greater safety than if he had been traveling alone.

Going on foot, Falk takes a long time to reach the Şhing. But he has been well prepared. Zove's House does not lack pleasant and useful devices, some of them technologically advanced. Most importantly, however, it contains a library in which Falk finds the *Tao Te Ching*. Le Guin never refers to the book by name, but she quotes from it fairly frequently (in her own version, a combination of several translations). All the really good people in the novel know the *Tao Te Ching* and quote from it. Some of the less good people steal Falk's copy, and the Prince of Kansas, who is noble, if slightly insane, gives Falk a copy to replace the stolen one.

Certain passages from the *Tao Te Ching* are appropriate to Falk's situation. Thus, he quotes to the old Listener he meets in the forest:

> Everyone is useful
> only I alone
> am inept
> outlandish.
> I alone differ from others
> but I seek
> the milk of the Mother
> the Way. . . .

It is true that Falk is outlandish, for he was not born on Earth, and at this point he does not know *where* he comes from. He is seeking the truth from liars, and his only hope of obtaining it is by being absolutely truthful himself. "In following the Way, the way is lost," the Prince of Kansas tells him. He hopes to obtain truth by being truthful, yet he is easily fooled by the tool of the Shing, Estrel, whom he loves and trusts until he is forced to disbelieve her. And yet he does find the Way; although misapplied to Estrel, love and trust do fortify Falk's soul and help him find the Way and to reach his goal—Es Toch.

It is by dint of studying the first words of the first chapter of the *Tao Te Ching* that Falk prepares to retain his identity when he is about to be turned back into Ramarren.

> The way that can be gone
> is not the eternal Way.
> The name that can be named
> is not the eternal Name.

Sitting in his room alone, waiting for the mysterious operation that the Shing are about to perform on him, Falk mesmerizes himself by repeating these words over and over again. He is trying to keep his identity as Falk, and therefore his name, so it is mystically correct that to do so he concentrate on the eternal Name. To follow his way, he must remember that it is not the eternal Way. These mystical insights outwit the lie by going beyond truth and lies to the paradox of what can only be *known* and not talked about, except in the most abstruse and riddling manner.

The *Tao Te Ching* works like a charm, like magic. This fact looks forward to *A Wizard of Earthsea*, wherein names, although perhaps temporarily unknown, do not lie somewhere beyond knowledge. The magic of Earthsea depends on what is fully understood, not on what lies beyond reason. Falk-Ramarren enters a metaphorical darkness at the beginning of *City of Illusions* and a literal darkness when he leaves the Earth for the stars. And he finds the way to that second darkness by the darkness of the *Tao Te Ching*, the riddles set by an ancient civilization to cure those who know, or think they know, too much, of pride in knowledge. Darkness in *City of Illusions* is not the darkness of evil, as in *A Wizard of Earthsea*, but the darkness of mystery, as in *The Left Hand of Darkness*.

Le Guin enjoys sending people into the unknown. And if she can send them into the unknown *from* the unknown, so much the better. Rocannon goes on a journey across a partially unexplored planet and is continually surprised by what he finds. So is the reader. Falk journeys across an America returned to wilderness and is continually surprised by what *he* finds. Again, the reader is too.

Le Guin's primary enjoyment when writing a book is "the chance to take another journey," and she is far more concerned about this than about plots. But she is too modest if she suggests that she is unconcerned about the way she tells a story. Le Guin keeps the reader continually wondering what will happen next, while giving him enough clues to make each event ultimately appear inevitable. Fantasy and science fiction provide her with opportunities to tell a good story filled with suspense, excitement, plenty of marvels— and to convey a message at the same time. The limitless possibilities of these genres are probably one of the reasons why she is so attached to them.

Throughout these three early novels there are hints of two other races out in space, the Hainish and the Cetians. Le Guin will continue to refer to the Hainish and the Cetians in her later science-fiction novels, with the exception of *The Lathe of Heaven*; so it is worthwhile to take note of what she says about them here. The Cetians are mentioned more than once for their skill as mathematicians. In *Rocannon's World* the Faradayan rebels whom Rocannon hears on his radio use Cetian numerals, as do all the members of the League of All Worlds. However, the Shing do not use Cetian mathematics, which convinces Falk-Ramarren that they are indeed alien.

The Cetians have less power and prestige than the Hainish. Rocannon is of Hainish extraction, having been adopted by his Terran father. He was born on Hain (which Le Guin also calls Davenant). When he walks into a room full of the Winged Ones, it reminds him of walking through a museum full of statues of the ancient Hainish gods. In *Planet of Exile*, a mural that Rolery sees in Landin includes a picture of the Great Hall of the League on Davenant. This gives us the clue that the Hainish organized the League of All Worlds.

The last reference to the Hainish in these early novels comes in *City of Illusions*, where we see a patterning frame.

> Thought to have come originally from the great culture of Davenant, though it was now very ancient on Earth, the thing was a fortune-teller, a computer, an implement of mystical discipline, a toy.

Consisting of beads strung on wires within a frame, it is a cousin of the abacus. It is not used for counting, however, but for identifying Falk as a visitor from outer space. Like the Taoist sayings, it has the charm of what is strange and mystical and yet is made up of familiar elements. Le Guin excels at the invention of situations and objects that exemplify this kind of blend, and we shall see this talent of hers at work in the Earthsea trilogy, with its very convincing magic, and in *The Left Hand of Darkness*. But the scope of such invention is quite limited in her early works.

Rocannon's World, Planet of Exile, and *City of Illusions* rely heavily on standard science-fiction ploys—faster-than-light ships, life on other worlds, physical differences between Earthmen and aliens, mysterious psychic powers, colonization of other worlds, intraspecies battles, and galactic empires. But they also explore choice and freedom, and enemies within as well as enemies without, as George Edgar Slusser points out in his *Farthest Shores of Ursula K. Le Guin* (1976).

In *A Wizard of Earthsea* and *The Left Hand of Darkness,* Le Guin's next two novels, her writing is considerably more subtle and complex and relies less on science-fiction tricks. In fact, in the Earthsea trilogy she does not rely on them at all, because the basis of the Earthsea trilogy is magic. She continues to explore choice and freedom, enemies within and enemies without, and she continues to send her characters on journeys. As she goes on, the connection between the outer journey and the inner journey becomes much more apparent.

3

The Earthsea Trilogy

journeys and marvels: these remain. The Taoism, too, remains, because that is something really essential to Le Guin's view of life, and it recurs throughout her work. Journeys and marvels are quite consistent with Taoism. Legend has it that Lao Tse disappeared from sight, at the end of his life, while on a mysterious journey, and later Taoists were alchemists and magicians. But it is not Taoist magic, which was largely sexual and concerned with obtaining long life, that Le Guin describes in the Earthsea trilogy. Searching in her unconscious and relying on impressions of magic received from her reading in childhood, she comes up with a type of magic more consistent with the teachings of Lao Tse than the Taoist magic actually was.

Rocannon and Falk-Ramarren both evolve extraordinary powers that are easy to take quite literally and that satisfy the wish for the marvelous in a fairly rudimentary way. In the Earthsea trilogy, marvels are there from the very beginning, and at the end of each journey is the goal of greater psychological maturity. And there is magic, too, in abundance—magic that is governed by the laws of the psyche.

Le Guin was not writing for young children when she wrote these fantasies, nor yet for adults. She was writing for "older kids." But in fact she can be read, like Tolkien, by ten-year-olds and by adults. These stories are ageless because they deal with problems that confront us at any age. They are about attaining maturity and self-knowledge, a theme for which we are never too old. As long as we truly live we grow, and as long as we grow there is room for greater self-knowledge and for new dimensions of maturity.

In her essay, "Dreams Must Explain Themselves" (1973), Le Guin tells us what she set out to say in the Earthsea trilogy:

> The most childish thing about *A Wizard of Earthsea*, I expect, is its subject: coming of age. . . .
>
> The subject of *The Tombs of Atuan* is, if I had to put it into one word, sex. There's a lot of symbolism in the book, most of which I did not, of course, analyze consciously while writing; the symbols can all be read as sexual. More exactly, you could call it a feminine coming of age. Birth, rebirth, destruction, freedom are the themes.
>
> *The Farthest Shore* is about death. . . . It seemed an absolutely suitable subject to me for young readers, since in a way one can say that the hour when a child realizes, not that death exists—children are intensely aware of death—but that he/she, personally, is mortal, will die, is the hour when childhood ends, and the new life begins. Coming of age again, but in a larger context.

Because each of the novels in the Earthsea trilogy represents a coming of age, each of them is told from the point of view of the boy or girl who is achieving this goal, starting with the young wizard Ged in *A Wizard of Earthsea* and then going on to the young priestess Tenar in *The Tombs of Atuan* and the young prince Arren in *The Farthest Shore*.

Le Guin started writing the Earthsea trilogy by a kind of chance, not because she was convinced that she had a message for today's youth. In 1967 the publisher of Parnassus Press asked Le Guin to write a book for older children, giving her complete freedom of approach. She was delighted. For a truly creative mind, an outside stimulus very often provides the needed incentive to explore new dimensions of the imagination. This was certainly the case with *A Wizard of Earthsea*.

As she thought of a subject, she went back to two of her earlier stories, both of which have since been reprinted in *The Wind's Twelve Quarters*. "The Word of Unbinding," published in 1964, describes a wizard who has been captured by an enemy from whom he cannot escape. He chooses to die in order to enter the land of the dead, which is the only place where he can defeat his enemy, who owes his uncanny power to the fact that he can *return* from the dead. Already, this story looks forward to *The Farthest Shore*, but in the Earthsea trilogy it is no longer necessary for a wizard to die to enter the land of the dead. The other story, "The Rule of Names" (1964), posits a fundamental rule of Earthsea magic—one that Le Guin had learned as a child from Lady Frazer's *Leaves from the Golden Bough* (1924): to know the true name of a person is to have power over that person.

The action in both stories takes place on islands; this inspired Earthsea, which is an archipelago. When Le Guin considered magic, she began to wonder about wizards and what they did before they became aged Gandalfs. Did they go to college? Pursuing this idea for her new book, she began to see where her young wizard could go, and she drew a map and named the separate islands. She also named her wizard: Ged.

Ged is his true name. It was given to him at his rite of passage into manhood at the age of thirteen, by the mage Ogion. He has to keep it secret from all except those he trusts absolutely. It is the secret of his identity and helps him use his native power. The true name is a source of power, and the knowledge of its gives power not only over people but over animals and things.

Before the young wizard became Ged, while he still went by his boy's name of Duny, he had learned from his aunt, a witch, the true names of various birds of prey. Calling them by their true names, he could summon them from the sky, thereby earning his use-name of Sparrowhawk. But in order to become a wizard, he must learn many more true names than a village witch can teach him, and he must also learn when and how to use this knowledge. What this book is really about, from start to finish, is naming and being named. Ged has to handle words in such a way that they identify the inner reality of what he is naming and, by naming, controlling.

Le Guin comments that this makes her wizard, in one aspect, an artist. In fact, magic in the Earthsea trilogy is both a science and an art. The scientific side of her magic is connected with the view of magic as an early but mistaken form of science, as expressed by Sir James George Frazer in *The Golden Bough* (1911–15). A critic, T. A. Shippey, has commented on this similarity and also on the way in which Le Guin differs from Frazer. The magic of Earthsea, while similar to some of the practices Frazer describes, is effective, not mistaken. It can be learned like a science. But although much of the learning consists of memorization, it is useless to teach magic to those without the power to use it. This provides another reason for saying that the wizard is like an artist.

Ged has that power to an exceptional degree. When he is still a child, before he has any training in magic, he repeats a charm that he had heard his aunt use to call a goat—so effectively that all the goats he is herding gather around him and will not disperse until his aunt says another charm. This episode influences her to teach him magic, as she sees that he has power. Indeed, she will soon find out that he has so much power that he frightenes her.

The incident with the goats, reminiscent of the Sorcerer's Apprentice, is revealing because over the course of *A Wizard of Earthsea*, Ged makes more and more serious mistakes by using spells that are too advanced for his power—until he is almost destroyed by them. Working against the development of his power are serious flaws of character, pride and temper, which he has to learn to control in order not to

endanger himself and those around him. But in his boyhood
he knows of no drawbacks to his power and learns everything
he can from the witch. He achieves fame on his native island
of Gont by defending his village from attackers from Karego-
At in the Kargad Empire, using an illusion spell to fool them
with shapes in the fog. This feat brings Ogion to him, who
says that it is dangerous "to keep dark the minds of the
mageborn." Ogion gives Ged his true name and takes him
as his apprentice.

Ogion is a mage of great power, famous for having
tamed an earthquake; but he speaks and acts little. In this,
he is a true Taoist sage. The *Tao Te Ching*, in passage after
passage, teaches the wisdom of refraining from action and
speech unless they are absolutely necessary. Again, as in
Planet of Exile, Le Guin is expounding on the virtue of *wu
wei*. But Ogion, a man of power, is a far more convincing
example of *wu wei* than Rolery, who can easily be seen as a
traditional woman who leaves action to the men. Ogion tries
to teach Ged to have respect for the living things around
him and not be forever thinking of ways to *use* them. He
also tries to impart to Ged his own reluctance to use power
unless it is absolutely essential. But since Ogion teaches by
example rather than by spelling things out, Ged, despite his
native intelligence, does not understand and only believes
he is learning when Ogion teaches him runes.

Ged has not been long with Ogion when he makes
another serious mistake stemming from his lack of understanding. On his rambles through the fields of Re Albi,
where Ogion lives, he meets the daughter of the local lord,
who asks him questions about what he can do. Eager to
impress the girl, Ged boasts of his powers. When she asks if
he can summon the spirits of the dead, he claims that he
can. He also claims to be able to change his shape. When he
returns to Ogion's house, his mentor is not home; Ged takes
down the lore-books that Ogion has never opened in front
of him and looks for a spell of self-transformation. Instead,
he comes across a spell for summoning the spirits of the

dead. He feels horror at the spell, but cannot keep from reading it through. When he has finished, the room is dark, and there is a shapeless shadow crouching by the door, whispering to him. Ogion enters, a white radiance burning around him and his staff, and drives the shadow away.

For the first time in this book, we witness the battle between light and darkness, which recurs throughout the Earthsea trilogy. Here, light and darkness stand for good and evil, as they do traditionally. They also represent the polarities of life and death, knowledge and ignorance, wisdom and stupidity, the power to act and the impotence of possession. What they do *not* stand for is God and the devil, concepts that are absent from the Earthsea trilogy.

Some of the inhabitants of Earthsea believe in gods, but the peoples of the Inner Lands, where Ged lives, believe only in magic. In *The Tombs of Atuan*, we learn that the inhabitants of the Kargad Empire believe in two sets of gods: the Godking, who is a deified living ruler, and the God-Brothers, about whom little is said. They also believe in the Nameless Ones, dark powers that existed at the beginning of the world, before the light came. Worship of the Nameless Ones has fallen into decay, which is just as well; Le Guin states that they are the real evil powers that it is wrong to serve.

The Godking and the God-Brothers, however, are not represented by Le Guin as real gods, any more than are the idols of the people living out on rafts whom Ged meets in *The Farthest Shore*. Even the being who created Earthsea, Segoy, several times referred to in *The Farthest Shore*, seems to be not a god but the first mage. The Earthsea trilogy is an atheistic fairy tale. But the struggle between the powers of the light and of the dark is taken with quite as much seriousness as if Le Guin were a Christian.

Le Guin's ideas about the relationship between light and darkness are subtly different from those of a Christian. We get a first hint of her attitude in Ogion's remonstrance to Ged, after he has saved him from the shadow by the door.

Ged, listen to me now. Have you never thought how danger must surround power as shadow does light? This sorcery is not a game we play for pleasure or praise. Think of this: that every word, every act of our Art is said and is done either for good, or for evil. Before you speak or do you must know the price that is to pay!

This is something like the Christian idea of the prevalence of sin. The Christian believes he is saved but is at the same time aware that he is liable to continue to sin as long as he is alive. This is why he prays not to be led into temptation. The intimate connection between good and evil suggested by the simile of shadow and light is closer to the Taoist belief in the inseparablity of opposites than it is to Christian dualism.

Ged has been warned of the danger that accompanies power and has had it demonstrated to him in no uncertain fashion. But he is still not convinced. Ged is obstinate, as well as proud and hot-tempered, and he will have to make the same mistake again and again before he fully accepts the truth of Ogion's warning. For the time being he sulks. He accuses Ogion of teaching him nothing, and Ogion gives him leave to go to the school for wizards on Roke Island. Ged chooses to go, although he knows that he loves Ogion.

Love does not come easily to Ged. He lost his mother early, his father was harsh with him, and his aunt valued him only for his magical power. Later, when he meets Vetch at the school for wizards and Vetch offers him an unshakable friendship, he will come to realize the meaning of love and its importance; but for the moment he renounces love easily for the sake of action and glory.

Ged goes to Roke accompanied by an evil omen. The ship that carries him there is called *Shadow*, and when Ged enters the school, although the light is behind him and an ordinary shadow would be cast in front, a shadow appears behind him instead. Entering the school is not easy, for he has to tell the doorkeeper his true name. When he finally leaves the school, he has to ask the doorkeeper for the doorkeeper's name in return, and the doorkeeper gives it willingly. We never see the doorkeeper doing anything but letting people in and out of the school, but he has to be a mage of great power to give away his name with so little fear. He is even more like a Taoist sage than Ogion, in that he appears to do nothing and teach nothing other than absolute trust; yet nothing can happen at the school without him. And when the other mages of Roke are losing their power and their presence of mind in *The Farthest Shore*, only the doorkeeper remains unperturbed.

He is one of the nine mages of Roke. After him come the Master Chanter, who knows all the old songs; the Master Windkey, who controls the weather; the Master Herbal, who teaches the properties of plants; the Master Hand, who teaches illusion; the Master Namer, who teaches long lists of true names; the Master Changer, who teaches true change as opposed to illusion; the Master Summoner, who teaches true magic, calling upon the deep powers of the universe; and the Master Patterner, who teaches the pattern behind things and how to make things whole. Superior to them all is the Archmage, the focal point for all the magic in Earthsea.

Ged learns his lessons well and quickly. But he still wants to learn too much too soon and is too eager to use his power. Like Ogion, the Master Hand warns him:

> The world is in balance, in Equilibrium. A wizard's power of Changing and of Summoning can shake the balance of the world. It is dangerous, that power. It is most perilous. It must follow knowledge and serve need. To light a candle is to cast a shadow.

But Ged is dissatisfied:

> Press a mage for his secrets and he would always talk, like Ogion, about balance, and danger, and the dark. But surely a wizard, one who had gone past these childish tricks of illusion to the true arts of Summoning and Change, was powerful enough to do what he pleased, and balance the world as seemed best to him, and drive back darkness with his own light.

These ambitious thoughts meet their punishment. Without realizing, Ged holds a darkness within him, the darkness of his rivalry with another student. After his first interview with the archmage on the day of his arrival, Ged is shown around the school by an older youth, Jasper, the son of a lord, and takes an instant dislike to him. The hatred and rivalry of the two youths grow. Finally Ged challenges Jasper to a duel of sorcery, even though he knows it is forbidden and his friend Vetch pleads with him to change his mind.

To show his power, Ged summons up a spirit from the dead, Elfarren, the most beautiful of women. She comes, looking sad and frightened, and with her comes a shadow like the shadow that had crouched beside the door in Ogion's house, which Ogion had banished with a word. But this time the shadow is blacker and stronger, and it leaps at Ged, wounding him almost mortally. The archmage Nemmerle saves Ged, but the feat saps Nemmerle of all his strength and he dies. Ged's anger and hatred and pride have led him to go too far once more, and it is the shadow of that anger and hatred and pride that wounds him. The shadow is really part of himself; but not even Gensher, the new archmage, fully realizes that. For the moment, the reader, too, is aware of the shadow only as a horror from another world, nameless and therefore immune from the power of magic.

Ged has a hard time recovering from his wounds and is greatly humbled by his disaster. He no longer believes that he can drive back darkness with his own light. He can only hope for a chance to undo what he has done, but the archmage Gensher tells him that is impossible. All he can do is stay on Roke for a while, behind the walls of spells that protect the island, and gather enough strength and wisdom before he leaves to keep the shadow from later entering into him and turning him into a *gebbeth*, a puppet of its will.

When Ged finally does leave Roke, he travels to a poor island, Low Torning, which is threatened by the dragon of Pendor and his brood. There Ged hopes to be safe and out of the way for a while. But the shadow comes back to haunt him—this time, when Ged does an act of kindness. He has made friends with a fisherman, Pechvarry, and tries to save Pechvarry's dying child even though he has been taught to let the dying spirit go. Once again he exceeds his own powers, and once again he puts himself in contact with the land of the dead.

The shadow reappears. It has been waiting for Ged at the wall of stones that separates the land of the living from the land of the dead. This time, Ged manages to shake off the shadow, because his act of hubris had been in the service of love rather than of envy and hate. For a moment his staff blazes with light. Suddenly Ged falls into a catalepsy and the *otak*, the little wild beast that he had made into a pet at Roke, brings him back by licking him. Love, even the love of an animal, has saved him.

He decides to face the dragon of Pendor immediately, while he still can. It seems to him, in fact, that this is the one thing he can and must do. He is already realizing the truth of a statement the Master Summoner had made to him while he was still on Roke. The older wizard had told him that, as a man grows in power and knowledge, he finds himself faced with ever more limited choices until he ends up doing only what he must do. This distinctly Taoist aphorism is so important to Le Guin that she has Ged repeat it, in different terms, to the young prince Arren in *The Farthest Shore*. Ged will tell the prince:

> If there were a king over us all again and he sought counsel of a mage, as in the days of old, and I were that mage, I would say to him: My lord, do nothing because it is righteous or praiseworthy or noble to do so; do nothing because it seems good to do so; do only that which you must do and which you cannot do in any other way.

Ged is glad to go to meet the dragons, partly because he feels that the shadow will not follow him into a dragon's jaws. He is also curious to meet a dragon, after having studied their ways. And he is well rewarded, for the dragons

Le Guin has imagined are wonderful beasts, magical, wise, deceitful, and ruthless, with a strange, wild beauty all their own. They are very old and speak the Old Speech in which all magical spells are made, the language of true names.

Ged kills several of the younger dragons almost casually. But then he speaks to their father, who is ancient and huge. Ged hopes to control him because he has guessed the dragon's name. But an unexpected temptation awaits him. The dragon, once he knows that Ged has power over him through his name, offers, in return for that power, to tell Ged the name of the shadow that pursues him. If Ged knew that name, he could control the shadow. But the lad refuses the offer for the sake of the folk of Low Torning, who are in his charge. Instead, he makes the dragon swear that he and his sons will never come to the archipelago.

After this achievement Ged tries to go back to Roke, but the Roke wind, which keeps evil from the island, prevents him. He goes to another island, where he meets a man who tells him to go to the Court of the Terrenon, in Osskil. He sails to Osskil, and a seaman, Skiorh, leads him to the Court of the Terrenon. On the way, Skiorh is possessed by the shadow and attacks Ged, calling Ged by his true name to rob him of his power. Ged fights with him, faints, and then returns to consciousness within the Court of the Terrenon. The lady of the castle, Serret, the daughter of the lord of Re Albi, shows him the stone at the foundation of the castle, the Terrenon. She urges him to lay his hand upon it and ask it the true name of the shadow. But Ged knows the Terrenon is evil and will not touch it. Serret urges, "Only darkness can defeat the dark," but he replies, "It is light that defeats the dark."

Serret has tempted him with the power that will be his if he uses the Terrenon. Not only will he learn the name of the shadow, but he will become mightier in magic than the Archmage. She says that he will rule all men and she will rule with him. But her husband, Benderesk, is secretly listening to their conversation, and he steps out of his hiding

place to lay an evil spell on his unfaithful wife. Ged over-
powers Benderesk with the strength of his own will, breaking
the spell, and he and Serret hastily leave the Court of the
Terrenon to avoid Benderesk's vengeance. Ged has no
intention of linking his destiny to that of Serret, but neither
of them is safe in Benderesk's domain, even though Ged has
been able to withstand the evil enchanter for the moment.

Ged has been tempted again but has refused to yield. He
is beginning to learn. Serret can no longer influence him as
she had when they were both younger. Ged is coming to
realize the responsibility that goes with power, and how to
act on it. When he leaves the castle, no shadow waits for him
outside. Instead, there is a reminder of his folly in coming
to the Court on the advice of a man who was obviously not
a reliable guide: his little friend, the *otock* lies dead.

As Ged and Serret flee from the Court of the Terrenon,
Ged takes on the form of a hawk while Serret takes that of
a seagull. She is overtaken and torn to pieces by evil flying
monsters sent by her husband. But Ged flies straight on to
Ogion at Re Albi. Ogion changes him back and tells him to
hunt the shadow instead of letting himself be hunted. Ged
now has the strength to take the offensive, because he had
the strength to stand up to a dragon and to the enchanter
Benderesk. And perhaps this tactic will lead him to the
shadow's name. Ged takes Ogion's advice and pursues the
shadow—in a leaky boat that he has to patch with spells—
but the shadow eludes him. To avoid his pursuit, the shadow
tricks him with fog into being shipwrecked on a tiny island
where only two old people dwell. Ged loses the track of the
shadow for a while, as he has to stay long enough on the
island to make another makeshift boat. However, there are
indications that his luck is beginning to turn, for his shadow,
meaning only to shake him off, has done him a service. As
is often the case in Le Guin's works, good comes out of what
appears to be evil, as evil comes out of what appears to be
good. The old woman gives him half of the lost ring of
Erreth-Akbe (for which he will be seeking the other half in

The Tombs of Atuan). He accepts the object without knowing what it is. Then he goes after the shadow again, ending up with a better boat, the *Lookfar*, which he will keep through all his subsequent voyages. As Ged continues his search, he hears from people who have seen the shadow that it looks more and more like him—so much so that his friend Vetch, whom he meets on Iffish, momentarily does not know whether Ged is the shadow or himself.

Ged has a brief respite with Vetch and Vetch's brother and sister. He is very happy to be with Vetch's sister, who, apart from the enchantress Serret, is the only young girl he has ever known. He is able to relax and joke with her, and to talk to her of magic as she prepares provisions for Ged and Vetch to take with them in the boat—magic cannot supply food and drink. Vetch, who proved a fine friend on Roke by telling Ged his true name and by showing his trust in Ged at a time when the latter badly needed it, now tells Ged his sister's true name. And he insists on accompanying Ged on his hunt for the shadow.

The two sail far out into the ocean. Then land, the dry land of the shores of death, appears on the open sea before them. Ged gets out of the boat and goes to meet his shadow. It takes the form of all those with whom Ged has had a spoiled relationship—his father, Jasper, Pechvarry—and then turns into a beast, its orginal guise. Both the shadow and Ged speak the name "Ged" at the same time, and Ged's light and the shadow's darkness fuse. Thus Ged recognizes his shadow, naming it with his own name, and goes free. Vetch, looking on, sees what has happened:

> And he began to see the truth, that Ged had neither lost nor won but, naming the shadow of his death with his own name, had made himself whole: a man: who, knowing his whole true self, cannot be used or possessed by any power other than himself, and whose life therefore is lived for life's sake and never in the service of ruin, or pain, or hatred, or the dark.

When *A Wizard of Earthsea* was issued, it did not take critics long to point out that Le Guin was describing Jung's concept of the shadow. She was surprised by this, as she had never read anything by Jung, but when she did read Jung, she agreed. Le Guin has an extremely interesting essay, "The Child and the Shadow" (1975), in which she says that she first formed the notion of the shadow from a story by Hans Christian Andersen, but that this notion fits in with Jung's idea that we have to face up to our shadow. According to Jung, the shadow is made up of everything we have repressed in order to be "decent" adults. It should not be rejected; we need it as much as we need the light side of our selves. To Jung and to Le Guin, the shadow is a guide to our full potential.

This should prevent us from saying that now that Ged has recognized the evil in himself, he will do no more evil. He can still make mistakes—and in *The Farthest Shore* he will make yet another disastrous mistake—but he is not the servant of evil.

When we meet Ged in *The Tombs of Atuan* he seems mature, wise, and kind—like Ogion. However, he does not appear until nearly halfway through the book. *The Tombs of Atuan* centers around the young priestess Arha, whose true name, we learn from Ged, is Tenar. But the distinction between the use-name and the true-name is not as significant here as it was in *A Wizard of Earthsea*; we are no longer in the Inner Lands of Earthsea but on the eastern island of Atuan, in the Kargad Empire.

The people of the Kargad Empire have fair skins, unlike the inhabitants of the Inner Lands, and they have organized religion instead of magic. They despise and fear wizards, whom they do not consider to have immortal souls. Unlike the Kargs, who reincarnate, wizards are believed at death to change temporarily into ghosts and then to disappear altogether. The struggle between wizards and the Kargad priests dates back to the wizard Erreth-Akbe. Thar, the priestess of the God-Brothers, tells Arha about Erreth-Akbe's defeat at the hands of the high priest of the inmost temple of the Twin Gods, and about the breaking of his ring, half of which

remains in the treasury of the Tombs of Atuan. The other
half is now considered lost, after having been for a long
time in the possession of a kingly family that was overthrown
by the father of the present Godking.

Because no magic is practiced in the Kargish lands, there
is no need to conceal one's name. But the young priestess,
Arha, lost her true name at the age of six, when she was
dedicated to the Nameless Ones, the ancient dark powers.
The name Arha, meaning the Eaten One, signifies that she
is completely in the grip of the powers she serves and has no
individuality apart from them. She has been told again and
again since she first came to the sacred Tombs of Atuan as
a child, that from the beginning of time she has been Arha,
the nameless priestess of the Nameless Ones, continually
reborn as herself.

Arha lives in a sacred place, the Tombs of Atuan, location
of the Hall of the Throne, the temple of the Nameless Ones.
Nearby are the temple of the Godking and the temple of the
God-Brothers. As in the ancient days of the worship of the
Great Mother, only priestesses and eunuchs live within this
enclave. Le Guin does not tell us why men cannot take part
in the worship of these deities, but it is possible to surmise
reasons. The worship of the Nameless Ones is obviously very
ancient, so it is fitting that they should be worshipped in the
manner of the most ancient European and Asiatic religions,
and certain traditions of this ancient worship may have been
carried over to the adoration of the more recent gods. Then,
by describing priestesses robed in black and observing rites
associated with darkness, Le Guin may have been alluding
to the Yin symbol, which, in traditional Chinese thought,
represents darkness as well as femininity. Finally, subsequent
events in *The Tombs of Atuan* make it clear that Le Guin
wished to show what a sterile life is led by these women who
are cut off from contact with men.

She has no such prejudice against the life of men without
women. The mages and the boys they teach on Roke live
without women and manage very well. When a woman visits

Roke, some of the mages look at her askance, although the boys are thrilled. Danger has come to Ged from one woman—Serret—more than once. There are even two sayings in Ged's homeland, Gont: "Weak as woman's magic" and "Wicked as woman's magic." Although *The Left Hand of Darkness*, which Le Guin wrote after *A Wizard of Earthsea* and before *The Tombs of Atuan*, is a somewhat feminist book, the Earthsea trilogy does not seem very pro-female.

Arha dwells in a dry, dark place full of spiders and women clothed in black that reminds one of the land of the dead. There are no emotions in the land of the dead, and the priestesses of the Tombs pretend that they have no emotions. But the truth is that their emotions are stifled and repressed and find an outlet only in jealousy and rancor. Even worse for the priestesses than jealousy and rancor is their boredom.

The young priestess of the Godking, Penthe, who is a friend of Arha, says that she would sooner marry a pigherd and live in a ditch than be shut up in a desert where no one ever comes. And although Arha feels proud of her position as the one Priestess of the Nameless Ones, there are times when she is so bored that she can hardly stand it. She speaks about this to Manan, the eunuch who is her special guardian, and he tells her that in the olden days kings used to consult the Nameless Ones through their priestess. But now that there is a Godking ruling over the Kargad Empire, such consultations are not needed.

Just once, right after Arha has confessed her boredom to Manan, some visitors come to the Tombs. They are three prisoners, rebels against the Godking, who are sentenced to be sacrifices to the Nameless Ones. Arha condemns them to die of hunger and thirst in the dark, but she is tormented by her own decision. She believes in the Nameless Ones and desires to serve them, but is not cruel by nature. (Le Guin suggests that Arha received too much love from her mother in the first five years of her life to be permanently warped by her training as a priestess.) Arha wants to be strong and implacable but falls in a faint after issuing her dreadful decree. She becomes ill and has nightmares of having to bring food and water to the prisoners.

In order to condemn the prisoners, Arha, under the guidance of Kossil, the priestess of the Godking, has to enter the Undertomb, a very sacred place where men come only to die and where no light can be lit. Off the Undertomb is the Labyrinth, in which the treasury is concealed. Once Arha has gotten over her distress at the death of the prisoners, she explores the Undertomb and the Labyrinth, which she feels are her domain. She is all the more glad to go there when Thar, priestess of the God-Brothers, dies and she is left at the mercy of Kossil, who worships only power and would do away with Arha if she dared. Remaining in her own domain, Arha stays out of the way of Kossil and staves off boredom.

One night Arha goes into the Undertomb and finds a light there. Following the light, she finds that it radiates from a staff that a man is holding. She draws down an iron door that shuts the stranger in the Labyrinth. Peering down from a spyhole, she sees by the light of the staff the man standing before the iron door, trying unsuccessfully to open it with magic. Le Guin gives no explanation for this here, but simply shows the man's serenity in the face of defeat. Later she suggests that the Nameless Ones, working through the hands of their priestess, have the power to defeat Ged, in spite of his strength.

For of course the stranger is Ged. Although Arha does not know who he is, she does realize that he is a wizard from the Inner Lands, come to steal the ring of Erreth-Akbe. She is so thrilled by this realization that she laughs aloud. From the start, she does not react as the priestess of the Nameless Ones should. Even when she prays to her Masters for forgiveness for having seen their darkness broken and their tombs violated, something within her is glad of having seen life in the place of death.

The dialectic of life and death is the theme of the rest of

the book. It is Arha's duty to let the wizard perish of hunger and thirst in the Labyrinth. She even tells Kossil about the man in the Labyrinth, and when Kossil says he must be allowed to die there, Arha insists that she wants him alive. Her idea at that moment is to give him a quick, clean death; but as time goes on, she is kind to him in spite of herself. Arha needs him alive, although she does not realize it at first, because he gives meaning to the dreadful monotony of her days. She offers him water and food and her cloak to lie on and even takes him to the treasury, where he can find the half of the ring of Erreth-Akbe. (He has brought the other half with him.) She tries to keep all this a secret from Kossil, but Kossil is not easily deceived. Finally, she has antagonized Kossil so much that Ged tells her that she has to decide either to let him die and make her peace with Kossil, or to leave the Tombs of Atuan with him. She chooses to leave.

One cannot call her Arha once she is allied with Ged. The wizard, with his skill in discerning true names, gives her back her name, Tenar—the one she had before she was consecrated to the dark powers. And now she wears the ring of Erreth-Akbe, which Ged has made whole using a patterning spell. This ring, which is meant to be worn on a woman's arm, is marked with the lost rune of dominion and peace, the rune by which the kings of Earthsea once ruled. Ged came for the ring because he wants to be able to reinstate a king over Earthsea.

The dark powers try to hold their captives, but Tenar and Ged manage to escape. Ged has to kill Manan in the process, and an earthquake destroys the Tombs of Atuan behind them. Once they are free, Tenar, who feels guilty for having killed the three prisoners and responsible for the death of Manan, asks to be marooned on a desert island. Ged responds,

> You were the vessel of evil. The evil is poured out. It is done. It is buried in its own tomb. You were never made for cruelty

and darkness; you were made to hold light, as a lamp burning
holds and gives its light. I found the lamp unlit; I won't leave
it on some desert island like a thing found and cast away. I'll
take you to Havnor and say to the princes of Earthsea, "Look!
In the place of darkness I found the light, her spirit. By her
an old evil was brought to nothing. By her I was brought out
of the grave. By her the broken was made whole, and where
there was hatred there will be peace."

And so the two of them bring the ring to Havnor. But they
do not marry and live happily ever after.

Ged promises to visit Tenar whenever he can, but he
cannot stay with her, because he has things to do that he
must do alone. Tenar is so resentful at this that for a moment
she wants to kill him. Their relationship is deep and complex.
Ged draws her away from her life as a girl among women
and makes her break all the laws she had been taught to
believe—Ged even kills Manan, the one person who had
always loved and been kind to Tenar. The reader may share
Tenar's disappointment that they are not going to marry,
but such a reaction is absurdly traditional in the context of
this tale. How can Tenar marry anyone? She is not complete;
she has never learned to be free. She has to learn to go her
own way before she can give herself completely to anyone.

It is true that by consenting to leave the Tombs of Atuan
with Ged, Tenar has entrusted herself to him. But she does
not truly know him. Throughout most of their interactions,
Ged has been unusually passive, waiting patiently to see
whether she will kill or save him. He has spoken to her of
his deeds, but that is not the same as seeing them. And he
has a need to be alone. Tenar has given herself to Ged, but
he gives her back to herself—to learn freedom, a heavy
burden. Ged takes her to his master Ogion, who will help
her find her own way. So if independence lies before Tenar
instead of marriage, perhaps this book is more feminist than
it appears.

There is another side of this matter—Ged's. Before he
comes to Atuan, there is no woman in his life. At the end of

A Wizard of Earthsea, it looks as though Ged will marry Vetch's sister. But there is no mention of her in *The Tombs of Atuan*, and in *The Farthest Shore* we learn that she is married to a carpenter. She needed a home and a family, not the wandering life that is all Ged has to offer; for Ged has no possession but his staff and has to rely on others for his daily bread in return for magic. Besides, although she is a wizard's sister, there is no wizardry in her.

"Like knows like," as Ged says to Akaren in *The Farthest Shore*. Tenar, even though the powers she served are evil and not worth anyone's worship, is nevertheless a priestess, and has the power that goes with her office. Ged cannot leave the Labyrinth without her, nor can she leave the Labyrinth without him. He is very patient with her, and does his best to please her, even when she is threatening him with death. He even courts her by clothing her, with his magic, in a beautiful dress, but returns her to her customary black when she objects. But Ged truly wins her when he calls her Tenar, bringing back unconscious memories of her mother, who loved her so tenderly. After he has re-named her Tenar, she dreams of her mother, in the form that she ascribes to the dead of the Inner Lands. In this way, she realizes the connection between her mother's love and Ged's. And in *The Farthest Shore*, before Ged comes to Selidor, the two people he wishes to see once more are Ogion and Tenar. So there is love, even if there is no marriage.

The Farthest Shore is the strangest book of the trilogy. In it, although Ged has become Archmage and should therefore be a Taoist sage, he does a lot of talking. In the British edition of *The Farthest Shore*, Le Guin changed three long passages because she was told that Ged was talking too much. Her first instinct was to let him talk, because she was so anxious to convey her thoughts on a very difficult subject, the acceptance of death as a key to living joyously. She manages this even though, not believing in immortality, she tells her reader that "the dead drink dust" and do not feel any emotion, engage in any activity, or see the light of the sun. The only positive trait she attributes to them is that they rest in peace. T. A. Shippey points out that this conception of the dead owes much to the poet A. E. Housman, who says, in *A Shropshire Lad* (1896):

> In the nation that is not
>   Nothing stands that stood before;
> There revenges are forgot,
>   And the hater hates no more;
>
> Lovers lying two and two
>   Ask not whom they sleep beside,
> And the bridegroom all night through
>   Never turns him to the bride.

In the Earthsea trilogy, the dead inhabit a dry land that is always dark. It is silent and still, with unchanging stars above. A low wall of stones separates the living from the dead, and there is a slope leading downward from that wall into the land of the dead. A living mage can descend that slope and return, but even for him the ascent is difficult. After death, no one comes back across the wall unless summoned by a mage. Very far down at the foot of the slope is a dry river, and beyond it are the mountains of pain, which cannot be crossed by the dead.

This landscape owes much to another poet, Rainer Maria Rilke, who, in the tenth poem of his *Duino Elegies* (1922), describes a town where all the values are false because the inhabitants deny death and look only for distractions and satisfactions. But beyond it are the Laments, personified as women, who greet the newly dead and show them their new land. They point out the new stars above, and the mountains where pain was once quarried. At the foot of the mountains is the spring of joy, which among living human beings flows mighty as a river.

By this spring of joy, Rilke means that the acceptance of death is necessary for the living to find true joy in life. Le

Guin does not keep the spring of joy in her portrayal of the land of the dead. For it she substitutes the dry river. There is a grim finality to her conception of death that goes beyond Rilke's poetic ambiguities. But like Rilke, whom she acknowledges as an influence, she believes that accepting death brings joy and denying it destroys joy. Le Guin does not immediately explain her viewpoint in *The Farthest Shore*. She simply shows that all over Earthsea the joy has gone out of life and the power of magic is dwindling. The disappearance of magic is a true disaster in the islands of Earthsea, where "the uses of magic are as needful to their people as bread and as delightful as music," and it is with this news that the book begins.

The young prince of Enlad, who is the descendant of Morred, a mage and hero from very long ago, travels to Roke to tell Ged that magic is failing on Enlad, and to ask for a remedy. The same news has come from other places, and Ged decides to venture in search of the cause, even though all seems well on Roke. He takes with him the young prince, whose use-name is Arren and whose true name is Lebannen. He does not tell the other mages why he is taking Arren, but we learn at the end of the book that it is because he has recognized in him the king who will rule over all Earthsea, by the power of the ring of Erreth-Akbe, and of whom it has been prophesied that he will cross "the dark land living and come to the far shores of the day."

Arren is glad to go with Ged, and they set out in the boat *Lookfar* without any very clear purpose except to go to Hort Town and ask for news. Once more Ged is on a journey at sea in pursuit of something that he does not know. But this time he is no longer young, and he brings a companion, whose youth and spirit he has to use. Ged lays a heavy burden on Arren, and Arren nearly breaks under it, but the fact that he does not break shows his fitness to be king.

Ged and Arren find Hort Town to be an evil place. Drug addicts sit in the market with flies buzzing around their lips; the goods sold are shoddy; there is no regard for law and order; and in spite of the bright colors of the town, it seems unreal. The people there deny all knowledge of magic, but Ged manages to contact Hare, a wizard who had worked for the pirate Egre until his magic ran out and Egre cut off his right hand. Incoherent with *hazia*, the drug to which he is addicted, Hare rambles on, but manages to convey that he has given up his name and his power to escape death. Suddenly, the pirate Egre arrives, knocks Ged over the head, and takes Arren captive to sell as a slave. When Ged comes to, he rescues Arren, and the two resume their course in *Lookfar*. This episode is exciting, but, from the point of view of their search, a vision that Arren has just before his capture is more important—a vision of a lord of shadows, offering a tiny light. Apparently this vision helps Ged more than Hare's ramblings.

Arren has no more visions as they sail along, but he has dreams. His dreams continue throughout their journey, and they are dreams full of his horror and fear of death and his susceptibility to the gift of immortality, which someone in his dreams offers to him. These dreams are the burden that is laid on Arren, which Ged, who cannot hear the tempter because he does not desire anything beyond his art, uses to find his way to the source of the troubles in Earthsea. Someone is deliberately sending these dreams to all the men of power, playing on the weakness that permits them to hear him. The enemy without speaks to the enemy within. Behind all the failure of joy and magic in Earthsea is a man whom Ged had believed dead, a man with the power of a great mage. His use-name is Cob, which means spider. Before leaving Roke with Arren, Ged had said to the Master Patterner, watching a spider in the grass, that evil is a web men weave. It turns out that Ged himself has had a hand in weaving the evil that has come upon Earthsea.

Years earlier, Ged had been offended by Cob's skill in bringing the spirits of the dead among the living, as a kind of trick to amuse people, and Ged punished him by forcing him to go into the land of the dead himself, even though

Cob was desperately afraid of death. Ged had acted in anger and pride, the old shadow side coming out again, and had done wrong. Self-righteously, he punished Cob for his own faults, and now Ged again finds himself trying to set right a prior wrong. He says to Arren, toward the end of the book, "What is a good man, Arren? Is a good man one who would not do evil, who would not open a door to the darkness, who has no darkness in him?" Ged had learned to accept his shadow as part of himself, in *A Wizard of Earthsea*, but this does not mean that he became perfect, in spite of the control he achieved over his own evil tendencies.

After Hort Town, the next place Ged and Arren come to is Lorbanery, famous for silk. But no more silk is woven there, and cobwebs cover the looms. The people who dyed the silk have gone mad, having given up their power in return for freedom from death. There is no more art or craft or magic on the island. For those who live on Lorbanery, everything has gone grey and indistinct. Ged talks to Akaren, the mother of the dyer Sopli, who says that she has revealed her true name and that words and names came out of her eyes and mouth "like spiderwebs." Ged restores her sanity by giving her a new name. He is able to do this because she regrets the bargain she has made and would sooner die than live as she does. But most of the people who have given up their power for immortality cling to their bargain and cannot be healed unless their tempter is destroyed. But first he has to be found.

Sopli says that the man they seek is in the west, and Ged takes him as a guide. Unfortunately, on their journey westward, Sopli drowns and Ged is badly wounded by some people on an island where he tries to land. Apparently the islanders have become so hostile that they now treat strangers as enemies. Sick at heart, feeling as if he were wrapped in cobwebs, Arren lets the boat drift. They are rescued by people who live on rafts out on the open sea, and remain with them until Ged's wound is healed. As in *A Wizard of Earthsea*, there is a time of respite here before the final journey. (Although Le Guin says she has not been overly influenced by Tolkien, she has learned his trick of balancing tension and release, as was already evident in the early science-fiction novels.) Then comes the festival of the Long Dance, and the people of the open sea, who had seemed impervious to the blight that had settled on Earthsea, are suddenly affected by it. The chanters are unable to sing throughout the night, as they should. Like Akaren and Sopli, who forgot their craft, the singers forget their songs. Only Arren is still able to sing, and he sings until dawn—one of the many indications of his great natural strength.

A dragon, Orm Embar, arrives at this point and asks for Ged's help against a new dragon lord who is destroying the dragons, taking away their speech and driving them mad. At last the guide they need has come. The story moves rapidly forward again, stopping only for a side glimpse at Roke, where things are going badly. When Ged and Arren arrive at Selidor, Cob confronts them. Armed with the steel staff of the Grey Mage of Paln, who first devised the spells that call the dead back among the living, Cob for a moment holds Ged captive. But the dragon throws himself upon the staff, sacrificing himself to save Ged, and crushes Cob.

Cob, who cannot be killed because he has a way of coming back from the dead, goes into the dark land. Ged and Arren follow him on and on until they come to the dry river. There Cob tells them that at the source of the river is the hole he has opened through which he passes from one world to the other, and which is drawing all the light out of the world. He half regrets what he has done but does not have the power to undo it. Cob is pitiable, and Ged seems to pity him, even as he works against him. As the *Tao Te Ching* puts it in chapter twenty-seven, a good man is a bad man's teacher and a bad man is a good man's responsibility. Ged accepts that responsibility by closing the hole and setting Cob free to die. There is even the suggestion that he has given back to Cob his true name, which Cob had forgotten.

But in performing this mighty feat Ged uses up all his power, and Arren has to help him the rest of the way. Ged and Arren struggle over the mountains of pain, on the far side of the dark land, until the mountains come to an end. There, beneath them, is the beach of Selidor. The oldest dragon of all, Kalessin, carries Ged and Arren back to Roke, where Ged kneels to Arren as his king. The dragon then carries Ged to Gont, where he will give up the life of action and merely *be*.

Two great acts of self-sacrifice, Orm Embar's and Ged's, have healed the world and restored its equilibrium. Had Ged and Arren not succeeded, even Roke would have been destroyed and the world would have come to an end. But now all is well, and a true king will reign in Havnor. It is remarkable that Arren reigns under his true name, Lebannen. This indicates that he has so much power that he can afford to let the whole world know his true name.

Ged had recognized that power from the start. When they were nearing their journey's end, he had said to Arren that he might achieve immortality if he desired it enough:

> There are two, Arren, two that make one: the world and the shadow, the light and the dark. The two poles of the Balance. Life rises out of death, death rises out of life; in being opposite they yearn to each other, they give birth to each other and are forever reborn. And with them all is reborn, the flower of the apple tree, the light of the stars. In life is death. In death is rebirth. What then is life without death? Life unchanging, everlasting, eternal?—What is it but death—death without rebirth?

In his desperate attempt to live forever, coming back from death each time he was killed, Cob had nearly destroyed the world. He had forgotten his own name and was persuading all the men of power to forget theirs. But what he had not understood, Ged tells him at the end, is that only names and shadows go into the dark land. The body lives on as part of all creation.

That is the only hope of life after death that Le Guin offers us at the end of this trilogy in which Ged has faced his shadow, his anima (or feminine archetype), and death in turn. In Jungian terms Ged performs the deeds that every man has to perform in the course of his life if he wishes to be whole. This is also a very Taoist, as well as a Jungian, conclusion. As Holmes Welch explains in his *Taoism: The Parting of the Way*:

> First, the mystic must know the eternal. When he knows it, he will rise to universal understanding; from universal understanding to breadth of personality, and so higher and higher until in the end he assumes the attributes of Tao itself. Then, being completely in tune with the order of the universe, what can harm him? To the end of his life there is no danger. Tao will never fail him. He knows the "sons"—the Ten Thousand Creatures—and, cleaving to their mother, Tao, he manages them. And when, sooner or later, he has to die, is it of any great consequence to him? From the height he has reached his point of view is exceedingly impersonal (though he feels compassion for those who die before they reach that height). His death will furnish physical and spiritual material for future lives. It is as acceptable to him as the fall of a leaf in autumn, whose rotting in spring will nourish the new bud. To the fact that this is the only kind of immortality he is completely reconciled.

In the last part of his life, having lost the magical power that was all he desired, Ged becomes a true Taoist sage, living only for contemplation. Completely reconciled to life and death, he disappears into the unknown, beyond the ken of all who knew him, like Lao Tse. The Earthsea trilogy is the work in which Le Guin has expressed her Taoism most artistically. It is also her greatest achievement, because the philosophical message is perfectly expressed in poetic metaphors that do not have to be recognized as metaphors by the reader but can be accepted simply as part of an exciting story. This means that someone who is reading purely for pleasure, without any thought of learning from a book, takes in her message almost unconsciously. In no other work of Le Guin's are form and content so completely inseparable.

4

The Left Hand of Darkness

here Ursula K. Le Guin picks up the thread of her early science-fiction novels. She takes a new look at the idea of a League of All Worlds, with its center on the planet Hain-Davenant. The League is no longer concerned with keeping off an enemy; the Shing have long since been defeated, and the worlds have formed themselves into an Ekumen, whose primary purpose is to facilitate trade and communication. Genly Ai, the envoy from the Ekumen to the planet Gethen, explains to Argaven, the king of Karhide, that the aims of the Ekumen are: "material profit. Increase of knowledge. The augmentation of the complexity and intensity of the field of intelligent life. The enrichment of harmony and the greater glory of God. Curiosity. Adventure. Delight."

The plot of *The Left Hand of Darkness* can be summarized quite briefly, although the book itself is not short. Told sometimes from the point of view of Genly and sometimes from the point of view of the Gethenian Estraven, the action is frequently interrupted by interpolated myths, legends, and reports on the planet Gethen, all of which serve to cast light on the events. But the events themselves are not numerous.

Genly Ai, a rather conventional young black man from

Earth, receives assistance when he first arrives in Karhide, from Therem Harth rem ir Estraven, the prime minister. However, Estraven falls from power and is exiled. Genly, who is implicated in Estraven's disgrace, feels betrayed by him. The envoy tries again to interest people in his mission, this time in the neighboring state of Orgoreyn, where Estraven has already sought refuge. There Genly is disowned by the faction that at first had supported him. Despite Estraven's warnings, he expected no betrayal, and he is surprised to be placed in a forced labor camp. He is rescued, again to his surprise, by Estraven. The two of them set out across a frozen wilderness to return to Karhide, and on the way real trust and love grow between them. However, there is a feeling on both sides that it would be inappropriate to express this sexually. They cross the Gobrin Ice that links Orgoreyn to Karhide at their northern points. Once they reach Karhide, Genly signals to the ship where his companions are waiting for him. The news of the Envoy's return and of the imminent arrival of the ship induces the government of Karhide to accept membership in the Ekumen. But Estraven is killed trying to cross the border back into Orgoreyn. Genly feels his loss very deeply. At the end of the book, Genly visits Estraven's family and speaks to them of his lost friend.

Is this a story of sublimated homosexuality? No, for the Gethenians are androgynous—an arrangement highly unusual in science fiction or out of it. Today, androgyny is a theme that has achieved a certain popularity, but when Le Guin published *The Left Hand of Darkness* in 1969, it was far from common. And yet her tale of a frozen planet of androgynous aliens who go into *kemmer* (as they call oestrus) once a month, becoming male or female through a chemical interaction with their partners, and are neuter the rest of the time, immediately struck the imagination of the reading public and earned her the Hugo and Nebula Awards. To achieve such success, Le Guin's ideas on androgyny must have fascinated a wide range of readers. Indeed, with the conflict that so often exists between men and women, it is possible to see Le Guin's vision of androgyny as pure wish fulfillment.

If there were no real distinction between women and men, there could be no fear, no arrogance, no mistrust between the sexes. There could be no double standard because there would be no second sex. At the same time, there would be no women feeling bitter because men had led them on with false promises or raped or otherwise exploited them. There would be no shame attached to pregnancy or burden attached to motherhood, since everyone at some time would be running the same risk. There would be no shame or hesitation about seeking sexual fulfillment, since the imperative nature of the biological need would be recognized by all alike. There would be neither sex roles nor stereotypes, so love could always be expressed physically in terms of the real nature of one's emotions. And everyone could have their turn at every form of procreation, begetting and giving birth. Old enmities and misunderstandings could be forgotten and there could be unity among people.

It is tempting to see androgyny as such a solution to the battle of the sexes. However, in her preface to the 1976 edition of *The Left Hand of Darkness*, Le Guin writes that she is not saying we will all be androgynous at some future date or that we all ought to be androgynous. Rather she claims that in some ways we already are androgynous. But women's dreams of fulfillment may have outstripped Le Guin's imagination. Many feminists have claimed that her androgynes are too male. This is quite possibly true. In her essay "Is Gender Necessary?" (1976), Le Guin comments that men more than women have been willing and able to imagine her androgynous aliens as men-women rather than effeminate men, and so make up for any failure of imagination on her part.

In the same essay Le Guin insists that androgyny is not

the main theme of the book, but rather fidelity and betrayal. Apart from the instantaneous response that the concept of the androgyne evokes in the reader's imagination, there has to be a reason, a reason that makes good sense in creative terms, for using the androgyne as the point of reference for a discussion of fidelity and betrayal. The androgyne, simply by being presented as existing, looks to the reader like the solution to a dilemma, and that solution looms so large that the theme of fidelity and betrayal tends to fade from view. If one investigates the full implications of *The Left Hand of Darkness*, fidelity and betrayal do in fact have importance, but they are not what strikes the reader at first glance.

The androgyne seems to a lot of us to be an answer. But, as the saying goes, "what is the question?" This whole issue of questions and answers is so important to Le Guin that she makes it a central feature of the Handdara, a mystical cult she has invented so that her androgynes can have a religion. (In fact, they have two; there is also the Yomesh cult, which is more important in Orgoreyn than in Karhide, where the story begins.) The Foretellers of the Handdara have perfected the art of accurate prediction in reply to any answerable question. Their visitor from Earth, Genly Ai, is fascinated by this skill and asks why more use is not made of it—for instance, for advising governments. The Foreteller whom he is questioning replies that they make these predictions purely and simply to show how useless it is to know the answers to the wrong questions. This seems to be a tenet of Le Guin's own philosophy. When faced with her androgyne, we have to ask the right questions. Perhaps, with this in mind, we should think again, and not assume too readily that the whole purpose of Le Guin's androgyne is to eliminate our intersexual conflicts on the most elementary level.

In "Is Gender Necessary?" Le Guin suggests some directions we could reasonably take in approaching this issue. When she first started to work with the notion of the androgyne, it was because Le Guin felt a need to define more exactly what gender and sexuality meant to her personally. Something was going on in the subconscious, for Le Guin and for many other women, which needed to be made conscious. Writing *The Left Hand of Darkness* was, she says, a kind of thought-experiment. By sending a conventional young man from Earth into a culture where there was no sexual differentiation, she made it possible for herself to imagine a kind of human experience in which sex roles played no part. She sums up the results of her experiment by saying that there is no war on her imaginary planet (although war is beginning to be a possibility) and no exploitation; sexuality is not a determining social factor. Finally, she concludes that, although an androgynous society would have problems (since all societies always do), our destructive dualisms, based on a structure of ownership and dominance would give way to a healthier, more integrated mode of life. In other words, the male-female aspect, instead of being in conflict, would be in harmony. We are alienated, in her opinion, because we have separated the yang (the masculine element) from the yin (the feminine element), and our greatest need is to bring the two together.

This suggests that the questions we could ask about the androgyne should be framed in psychological, philosophical, and even religious terms, rather than in terms of biology and desire. In fact, any reader of *The Left Hand of Darkness* who wants to know much detail about the biological functions of the androgyne is likely to be disappointed, since the basic information Le Guin provides on the subject is summed up in a couple of pages, in a style as blunt and dry as that of a medical text book. We hear far more about the myths and legends and religious beliefs concerning the androgyne than we do about his biology. (As it happens, Le Guin says "he" and "his" and refers to her androgynes as men, because "he" is the generic pronoun.) In those myths and legends, romantic love is very important. But there is far more explicit sexuality in the average women's magazine than in this book.

Although Le Guin insists that sex on her imaginary planet, Gethen, is remarkably guilt-free, this does not mean that the result is total license. She suggests various interesting reasons for this, but perhaps the most important reason is that her androgyne is a symbol of integration and wholeness. When she speaks of the alienation of the yang from the yin in our society, she is very serious, and she makes it quite clear in the course of her novel that the androgyne represents the coalescing of those two universal principles.

Toward the end of Genly's and Estraven's journey across the ice, the yin-yang symbolism is explained. Genly draws the ancient Chinese symbol of the double curve inside a circle, one half white and the other black. The white side stands for the yang principle, which is light, masculine, and active. The black side stands for the yin principle, which is dark, feminine, and receptive. The two sides together represent the reconciliation of opposites, conforming to each other's outline in perfect harmony. Repeating a line from an old Gethenian poem that Estraven had quoted to him earlier in their journey, Genly says, "Light is the left hand of darkness . . . how did it go? Light, dark. Fear, courage. Cold, warmth. Female, male. It is yourself, Therem. Both and one. A shadow on snow."

Patterns based on ancient Chinese thought are very important in this book. Le Guin acknowledges as much in "Is Gender Necessary?" and remarks that she had not been aware at the time she wrote *The Left Hand of Darkness* that the concept extends even to the Gethenian calendar, in which the current year is always the Year One. Yin-yang symbolism is absolutely basic to the traditional Chinese view of life, in which everything is a blend of yin and yang. A thing that has more yin qualities than yang qualities is considered yin, and vice versa; sometimes a balance can be struck between the two. This principle prevails in Taoism and in the *I Ching*, which was closely studied by Confucius, and to which Le Guin refers from time to time.

The *I Ching* consists of sixty-four hexagrams composed of solid (yang) and broken (yin) lines. The first hexagram in the book, Ch'ien, the Creative, consists of six solid lines. The second, K'un, the Receptive, consists of six broken lines. Male and female in their absolute state thus appear at the beginning of the *I Ching*, and all subsequent hexagrams represent the various combinations of these two elements. Everything is male-female in differing degrees. Each line in each hexagram has a special meaning, and one consults the *I Ching* to find the hexagram appropriate to one's situation by casting yarrow stalks or, more rapidly, coins.

Genly refers to this practice when he goes to consult the Foretellers of the Handdara and tries to understand how they arrive at their predictions and what chance they have of being right. As he wonders what question to put to the Foretellers in order to test them, he takes into account whether the Foretellers could give a yes-or-no answer to a question on a subject of which they were, in their normal state, quite ignorant. "This seemed to put the business on the plane of pure chance divination, along with yarrow stalks and flipped coins," he says. But he is assured that this is in fact not a matter of chance. This reference to the *I Ching* is doubly ironic, for while Genly is being ironic about yarrow stalks and flipped coins, Le Guin is being ironic about him and his attitudes, as she frequently is throughout the book. The would-be rationality that he brings to the subject of foretelling is typical of the defensiveness he exhibits until he finally learns to love and trust Estraven and, through him, Gethenians in general.

But the *I Ching* is not the main point at issue here, for the Handdara cult bears a very strong similarity to Taoism. The darkness it cultivates is the darkness of mystery, beyond all answers and solutions. As the Taoist places the highest value on the Void, the adept of the Handdara gives praise "to Darkness and Creation unfinished" and studies how to achieve ignorance. Such a goal is easily misunderstood by the would-be rational western mind, so Le Guin explains (although not immediately) what is meant by ignorance in this sense. It is "to ignore the abstraction, to hold fast to the thing." The entire training of the Handdara teaches the

adept to avoid looking for answers or even paying attention
to them once they have been given. "Nusuth"—"no matter"—is a typical Handdara response to most issues. Estraven,
who has received Handdara training, is remarkable in his
ability to react, immediately and with his whole being, in a
way that is totally appropriate to any given situation. In this,
he far surpasses Genly, who has to puzzle out the answer to
problems.

We could take this as a reference to feminine intuition,
but as an approach it is markedly Taoist. Taoism leans
traditionally toward the feminine (yin, receptive) and consequently has been in opposition to the philosophy of Confucius, which is more masculine and authoritarian. The political
systems of Gethen reflect the creative tension between
Taoism and Confucianism, since they are based on an
authoritarian form of government—monarchy or bureaucracy—that is modified by individual anarchism. The Gethenian is an instinctive anarchist—and so, according to Le
Guin, feminine—everywhere except in Orgoreyn, where
troublemakers are drugged and bullied into submission. The
Yomesh cult constitutes an aberration from the point of view
of the followers of Handdara, since it insists that all answers
were revealed in one revelation to its founder, the Foreteller
Meshe. As previously mentioned, the Yomesh cult is pre-
dominant in Orgoreyn. This is in itself significant. Karhide,
as the less power- and answer-oriented of the two states,
appears preferable to Orgoreyn. And yet it is from Karhide
that the first threats of real war on Gethen come, at the
moment when Estraven (who wishes peace) is overthrown
and proscribed.

Le Guin gets rather tired of people who overly discuss
her moral values and harp on her desire for wholeness and
balance. There is something peculiarly infuriating about
having glib lip service paid to values that have been worked
out through personal struggle and pain. And apart from
that, Le Guin, like any strong personality, has her dark side
and recognizes it in other people, including the people she

invents. A symbol of wholeness her androgyne may be, but the Gethenian is a human being and consequently is as subject to weakness, error, folly, and even crime. There is no war, but feuds and murder are fairly common. Every feature of Gethenian life is controlled by a stylized form of one-upmanship called *shifgrethor*, which is related to the Chinese concept of saving face, and which Genly, accustomed as he is to the masculine ego, finds baffling and extremely annoying.

Estraven, who is presented in the most sympathetic light as a truly admirable human being, capable of continence during *kemmer*, trained to perform enormous feats of strength and endurance through sheer will power, showing exceptional ingenuity and perseverance in the midst of every possible rebuff and failure, true to his purpose, to his love, and to his friend—this Estraven has, by the day of his death, committed every crime that the Gethenians most deeply despise. He is considered a traitor to Karhide because of his willingness to cede territory in a border dispute. In addition, he is so determined to help Genly in his mission that, in order to make Gethen join the Ekumen, he is willing to sacrifice the prestige (or *shifgrethor*) of Karhide. And since politics on Gethen is played on the level of *shifgrethor*, this is a very real betrayal from the point of view of Argaven, the king of Karhide. One might even say that betrayal runs in Estraven's family; one of his ancestors, whose tale is told in one of the "documents" with which the narrative is interspersed, was known as Estraven the Traitor for ceding territory in order to end a feud. The Estraven of the present story bears that ancestor's first name, Therem.

Even more deeply despised than betrayal is theft—and Estraven steals food, at the outset of their journey across the ice, to keep himself and Genly alive. The worst of all crimes is suicide, which Estraven commits by skiing straight into the guns of the border guards who have been posted to kill him. But perhaps most offensive from our non-Gethenian point of view is Estraven's incestuous love for his brother, to whom he vowed *kemmering* (or life-long fidelity) in their youth and with whom he has had a child. In itself, an incestuous relationship with a brother is permissible on Gethen, but the lovers are not allowed to vow *kemmering* or to remain together after the birth of a child. It seems that Estraven and his brother left their clanhome (or Hearth) after the birth of their child in order to preserve their relationship. The brother is now dead, possibly having committed suicide.

Incest, in fact, is a central theme in *The Left Hand of Darkness*, and it is largely in terms of incest that the idea of the androgyne is linked to the theme of fidelity and betrayal. Structurally, this is extremely important, because the basic situation on Gethen is somehow incestuous. At the beginning of the book, Estraven tosses off the epigram that "Karhide is not a nation but a family quarrel," but this turns out to be true. The basic social unit in Karhide is the Hearth, and every social institution on Gethen is based in some form on the Hearth—even the Commensality of Orgoreyn, which is a lifeless, loveless, schematized imitation of the close-knit, quarrelsome, loving, flesh-and-blood relationship exemplified by the Hearth. Gethenians share such an affinity in their basic outlook that sex between Gethenians must resemble sex between brother and sister (since Gethenians always mate as man and woman) more than any other sexual bond. Into this situation comes the alien, the stranger, and breaks the incestuous bond. Fidelity to the stranger means betrayal of the family.

The Gethenian myths and legends scattered throughout the narrative counterpoint the relationship between Genly and Estraven with a symbolism that reflects the details of their journey across the ice. This is particularly marked in "The Place Inside the Blizzard," the tale of incest that occurs, quite abruptly and unexpectedly, in the second chapter. At first it appears to have no connection with the preceding chapter, in which Genly records his belief that Estraven has let him down. But the juxtaposition of the themes of betrayal and incest, at the outset of the book, ensures that they will be connected in the reader's mind, although probably at the unconscious level. In the tale, two brothers vow *kemmering*, against the taboo. When a child is conceived, they are ordered to part, and the brother who bears the child commits suicide. The other brother, who is considered responsible for the suicide, is driven from the Hearth, but returns to curse it and announces that he too will commit suicide. He goes out on the ice and travels through a snowstorm until he reaches the place inside the blizzard where he no longer feels cold or pain and where everything, including himself, seems to be made of snow. Here his dead brother comes to meet him and says that this is the place where they will keep their vow. But the dead brother cannot speak the living brother's name, and this frightens the living brother, who says he will not stay and instead reproaches the suicide for killing himself instead of leaving the Hearth with him and keeping their vow in concealment. The living brother runs away and survives, although his left hand, which had been seized by the dead brother, is frost-bitten and has to be amputated. As an old man, shortly before his death, he takes back the curse from his Hearth, and reconciliation is finally brought about.

The next tale of prohibited love, in chapter nine, tells how Estraven the Traitor was born to the heirs of two feuding families and finally ended the feud, ceding land and killing some of his own clan. The heirs of the two families fall in love at first sight, apparently because they were fated to come together. The left and right hands of the ill-fated lovers and of the surviving parent and child match exactly, which proves (in emotional terms) their predestined affinity.

The last of these tales of love and death comes in chapter seventeen, where we get an Orgota creation myth. (In the first half of the book tales from Karhide are scattered through the narrative. Then in the second half Le Guin gives examples of the teachings of Orgoreyn, to strike a balance.) This myth tells how the first man kills all his brothers but one and couples with his surviving brother in a house built of the frozen corpses. Because his children are born in the house of flesh, each is followed around by a piece of darkness—his shadow. In the end, only darkness will remain. This myth counterpoints chapter twelve, "On Time and Darkness," in which the Yomesh belief is expressed that "in the sight of Meshe there is no darkness" and that there is no source or end.

The Gethenian myths and legends illustrate the theme of love, incest, and betrayal, while illuminating the interrelatedness of left and right, light and darkness, shadow and snow, birth and death, revelation and ignorance, beginning and end, and the denial of beginning and end. They are all summed up by a scrap of an old poem, *Tormer's Lay*, which Estraven quotes to Genly in chapter sixteen:

> Light is the left hand of darkness
> and darkness the right hand of light.
> Two are one, life and death, lying
> together like lovers in kemmer,
> like hands joined together,
> like the end and the way.

The first tale, the incest legend, remains dominant throughout *The Left Hand of Darkness*. Even as Estraven quotes *Tormer's Lay*, his voice shakes, for he remembers that in the letter his brother wrote him before his death he had quoted the same lines. When the two fugitives set out on their journey across the ice, Estraven tells Genly that the good weather tends to stay over the great glaciers, while the storms are pushed out to the periphery, and that this accounts for the legends about the "place inside the blizzard." This is a direct reference to chapter two and indicates that Estraven is going in search of his dead brother. He manages to find him, in chapter eighteen, when Genly teaches Estraven mindspeech and speaks Estraven's name, in mindspeech, with the dead brother's voice. This is particularly striking since, in the legend, the dead brother could not speak the living brother's name; and it implies that the curse of hopeless and prohibited love has somehow come to an end. Also left and right are affirmed by the quotation from *Tormer's Lay*, whereas in the legend the connection between left and right was destroyed when the living brother lost his left hand. Finally, in the last chapter, when Genly comes to Estraven's Hearth to speak of his dead friend to Estraven's parent and child, this represents a hope for new beginnings.

In *The Left Hand of Darkness*, Le Guin has told, in far greater complexity and ambiguity, substantially the same story as in *The Tombs of Atuan*. The sexual nature of the relationship between Genly and Estraven is blurred by the fact that Estraven is an androgyne who is neuter most of the time and Genly seldom has the opportunity to see him as a sexual being. But when he does, it is significant that he sees Estraven as a woman. As in *The Tombs of Atuan*, it is the "female" partner who contrives the male partner's escape. Genly, however, is very far from being the wise mage who serves the forces of light; and Estraven is by no means in the service of the powers of darkness. The latter represents, in his own being, the reconciliation of darkness and light. Finally, even less than in *The Tombs of Atuan* is there any living happily ever after, even without marriage. In order to complete Genly's rescue, Estraven has to die, and in order to bring his mission to a successful conclusion, Genly has to break his promise to Estraven to clear his name. Love, still the one necessity, is no longer a triumphant solution, but is in itself a source of grief and pain. And fidelity and betrayal take place on both sides.

The maturity of this conclusion to *The Left Hand of Darkness* leaves us in a chastened mood, no longer in the grip of the fascination we felt on first meeting the idea of the androgyne. Our longing for a lost completeness, for, as in the Platonic myth of the androgyne, the lost half of ourselves, our nostalgia for a once-upon-a-time when all went well—this may be a trap, a longing to regress to childhood with its latent sexuality and the closed circle of the family. But even within the family there is the "Other,"

and that other is a different human being, not just part of
ourselves. Only for the autistic child is there no one else to
relate to. As Estraven points out, duality is not unknown to
the androgyne, for there is always the Other. Recognition of
the Other is a lesson of childhood and maturity alike, and
we need this recognition for our psychological growth. Le
Guin's idea of androgyny leads toward a meeting of strangers
and of the sexes, not away from it.

In other words, Le Guin leaves us with an insight which
is as classical as her way of presenting it is unorthodox. This
is, basically, what makes of *The Left Hand of Darkness* a work
different in nature from other well-known thought-experi-
ments in human sexuality. When Aldous Huxley described
new types of sexual relationships in *Brave New World* (1932),
he was expressing quite directly his abhorrence of promis-
cuity and his angry regret that old sexual patterns were
changing. And when Joanna Russ wrote *The Female Man*
(1975), she was being just as direct about her resentment of
men and her approval of a world that would be full of
strong, healthy, happy, loving lesbians. Again, when Samuel
R. Delany describes, in *Triton* (1976), the dilemma of Bron
Helstrom, who is hopelessly confused about his sexual role
because he is looking for a woman who will conform to a
female stereotype that has long since disappeared, Delany
straightforwardly shows his disapproval of such nonsense.
When Bron Helstrom actually has a sex change in order to
turn himself into the kind of woman he thinks he wants and
then finds that the kind of man who wants that kind of
woman no longer exists (since he cannot be two people at
once), we do not feel sorry for him.

In fact, a comparison of *Triton* with *The Left Hand of
Darkness* is rather illuminating. The possibility of homosexuality as a man or a woman is open to Bron Helstrom, if he
feels incapable of a heterosexual relationship, and his possible homosexual partners are presented as kindly people
who are genuinely fond of him. Conversely, homosexuality
is to all intents and purposes ruled out in *The Left Hand of*

Darkness, although there is something called perversion on Gethen. Certain Gethenians remain in *kemmer* all the time and are called Perverts—quite logically, since constant *kemmer* suggests a sexual obsession that must be repulsive to those who are free from it. Without realizing it, Genly adopts this attitude, and when his companions finally arrive from their starship, he sees them as repulsively sexual.

Another contrast between the two books is that in *Triton* religion and politics are presented without much complexity, as part of the general mess in which Bron Helstrom finds himself, and their connection with his sexual dilemma is more or less coincidental. We have seen, on the other hand, that there is a close connection between the religion and politics of Gethen and the theme of the androgyne. The androgynes of *The Left Hand of Darkness* function within a whole and complete work of imagination that, unlike *Triton*, is not geared toward making a special plea for more liberal attitudes to sex. When Le Guin says that she is not proposing Gethen as an utopia and that she is not suggesting that we all become androgynes, except in so far as we already *are* androgynous, she is making an accurate statement.

Although the androgyne is very important in *The Left Hand of Darkness*, Le Guin invented Gethen, which she also calls Winter, before arriving at the idea that its people were androgynous. A year before she started work on *The Left Hand of Darkness*, she wrote "Winter's King," a short story in which the characters are mainly male. It tells how Argaven XVII, a promising young king of Karhide, is kidnapped by secret enemies. They manipulate his mind with drugs and induce a paranoia that would gradually turn him into a tyrant no longer loved by his people. Then he is turned loose in the streets of his capital, where he is found by a loyal subject and brought to the palace. Once he is sufficiently well to make decisions, he realizes what has been done to him and decides that he cannot remain king. Not being allowed to abdicate (he has been such a good king that the Council will not permit it), he seeks the help of the ambassador of the Ekumen and leaves Gethen in secret for Ollul, twenty-four light-years away. He arrives there still a young man. A Cetian doctor cures him of his induced paranoia, and Argaven XVII remains on Ollul for several years, studying subjects that will make him useful to the Ekumen. Then he returns to Gethen, arriving there sixty years after his departure, to find himself hailed as a deliverer by his former subjects, who now are rebelling against his son Emran. At the end of the story, he is shown bending over the dead body of Emran, whom he had last seen as a baby and who is now an old man. Faced with total defeat, Emran has committed suicide.

By the time this story was published, Le Guin had decided that the Gethenians were androgynous. So when "Winter's King" was published for the second time, in *The Wind's Twelve Quarters*, the necessary changes were made. In the new version, Le Guin referred to all her Gethenian characters as "she," while keeping titles such as "Lord" and "King." This was a deliberate modification of the practice of referring to them all as "he," which she had followed in *The Left Hand of Darkness*. In the note she attached to the story in *The Wind's Twelve Quarters*, Le Guin says:

> The androgyny of the characters has little to do with the events of this story, but the pronoun change does make it clear that the central, paradoxical relationship of parent and child is not, as it may have seemed in the other version, a kind of reverse Oedipus twist, but something less familiar and more ambiguous. Evidently my unconscious mind knew about the Gethenians before it saw fit to inform me. It's always doing things like that.

For the androgyny of the Gethenians to reveal its full implications, the relationship between Genly Ai and Estraven is necessary. This makes "Winter's King' and *The Left Hand of Darkness* two very different stories, in theme and in emphasis as well as in plot. But it is surprising how much of the way life is lived on Gethen appears in the short story. The bitter cold, to which the inhabitants are completely accustomed, is already present. So is the detail that fires are used, although the Gethenians know about central heating. The use of radio instead of newspapers and the use of slow-moving cars and ships powered by electricity indicate the Gethenians' ecologically sound use of their technology. Their vegetable food and their fondness for ale also appear, with the detail that the ale is liable to freeze over on cool mornings. The antagonism and rivalry between Karhide and Orgoreyn are also already present.

However, there are also differences. In "Winter's King" there are actual wars between Karhide and Orgoreyn, whereas in *The Left Hand of Darkness* there is only the possibility of war. Apparently "Winter's King" is situated historically some time after Genly Ai's visit, as there is a permanent representative of the Ekumen on Gethen. And while Le Guin says in *The Left Hand of Darkness* that all the kings of Karhide are mad, Argaven XVII is basically sane.

In both versions of the short story, as in the novel, the Hainish and the Cetians are present, in not too obtrusive a way. In "Winter's King," the ambassador of the Ekumen tells Argaven XVII that the inhabitants of the known worlds are all human, since they stem from the Hainish, who colonized a hundred worlds. In one of the "documents" in *The Left Hand of Darkness*, an early investigator notes that the Gethenians were probably the result of an experiment by the Hainish, who practiced human genetic manipulation in their colonies. At the same time, the investigator lets us know that this genetic manipulation also accounts for the Winged Ones of *Rocannon's World*. Such indications are typical of Le Guin, who has a tendency to get around any difficulties in logic that may arise in the course of her narratives by invoking the intervention of the Hainish. The Cetians, although appearing in the person of the doctor who cures Argaven XVII, have less responsibility placed on them. But their interest in physics is mentioned in "Winter's King," thus preparing the way for *The Dispossessed*.

However, it is the systematic working out of the contrast

between darkness and light, together with their basic oneness, that most strongly differentiates *The Left Hand of Darkness* from "Winter's King." We have seen that the adepts of the Handdara prefer darkness to light, while the followers of the Yomesh religion insist on light and condemn darkness. But light follows darkness and darkness light in spite of the preferences of the two religions. This is entirely in keeping with the principles of the *I Ching*, the most specific and detailed answers in which are given by what are called changing lines. A yang line changes into a yin line, at certain points in the hexagram, or a yin line into a yang line, leading one to a new hexagram. The light, masculine line becomes a dark line and the dark, feminine line becomes a light line. In this way one receives a double answer, which may be extremely complex and even apparently contradictory. Such mutability emphasizes the process of life, which is constant change. The genius of the *I Ching* is that it fits these changes into an ideational structure, so that life is not presented as meaningless flux.

The Foretellers of the Handdara go into darkness to find the answers to the questions that are put to them, but they come out of it into light to give their answers. When Faxe the Weaver, the leader of the group of Foretellers, answers Genly's question about whether Gethen will join the Ekumen, he appears as a woman clothed in light, with fire burning along her limbs. In contrast, in Orgoreyn, where the priests believe in total light and pour contempt on those who call upon the darkness, the reality of the state is to be found in the dark cellar, the prison, and the forced-labor camp. One cannot find it in the daylight.

Estraven himself, although an adept of the Handdara, sometimes uses "darkness" and "shadow" as negative terms. But he recognizes that shadow has to accompany light; as at a certain point in their journey over the Gobrin Ice, when he and Genly find that the lack of shadow on the snow makes progress difficult. Estraven even falls into a crevasse because he cannot see his way, and has to be pulled out by Genly.

Although Le Guin obviously prefers the Handdara and Karhide to the Yomesh religion and Orgoreyn, there is a strong message in *The Left Hand of Darkness* that dualism is a mistaken concept. This comes as something of a surprise to those who know the Earthsea trilogy, where light and darkness are clearly opposed. If light and darkness stand for good and evil in Earthsea, is Le Guin saying in *The Left Hand of Darkness* that it is impossible to distinguish between good and evil? It seems that the answer to this question is no. There is a clear distinction in *The Left Hand of Darkness* between good deeds and evil deeds. But what is more apparent in this novel than in the Earthsea trilogy is that good follows evil and evil follows good. As the *I Ching* teaches, no situation can remain at a state of climax but has to give way to its opposite. Good and evil belong together much more than some people suppose.

Le Guin gets annoyed when critics reduce the substance of her books to some simple message that she likens to "a fortune-cookie motto," but there is no denying that the simple message is there—that is, if one really wishes to boil one of her books down to a single sentence. One of the things we get from *The Left Hand of Darkness* is a parable about wanting one-sentence answers to the meaning of life. When Genly visits the Foretellers, he is told about the origin of the Yomesh cult. A certain lord once forced a group of Foretellers to answer the question, "What is the meaning of life?" The Foretellers took six days and nights to answer it. At the end, some were catatonic, some were dead, one had murdered the questioner, and the leader of the group, Meshe, had received the total insight that enabled him to found his cult. The adepts of the Handdara apparently find this story very funny, which, according to Taoist principles, they should. The Taoist who has received enlightenment does not go around making earth-shaking prophecies or founding cults, but is liable to say something quite ordinary, such as "Will you have a cup of tea?" But he does this in a way that is so totally appropriate to the situation that the person to whom he is offering the cup of tea is profoundly impressed and may even receive enlightenment, too.

5

The Dream

I n Guin's next two works, *The Lathe of Heaven* and *The Word for World is Forest*, show her coming much nearer home in time and space. *The Lathe of Heaven* is set in Portland, Oregon, Le Guin's home city, in the near future; and *The Word for World Is Forest* is based on the American war in Vietnam. The result is an increase in realism. Of the works she wrote up to 1973, Le Guin says:

> Along in 1967–68 I finally got my pure fantasy vein separated off from my science fiction vein by writing *A Wizard of Earthsea* and then *Left Hand of Darkness*, and the separation marked a very large advance in both skill and content. Since then I have gone on writing, as it were, with both the left and the right hands; and it has been a matter of keeping on pushing out towards the limits—my own and those of the medium.

Mindspeech does not recur in Le Guin's works after *The Left Hand of Darkness*, although George Orr, the hero of *The Lathe of Heaven*, has a capacity that is magical rather than scientific—his dreams come true. This is a proverbial expression for realizing one's fondest wishes, and yet it is felt by him as a curse rather than a blessing. While it is unlikely that Le Guin, with her dislike of dogmatism and allegory, would have let herself be influenced by C. S. Lewis, Orr's predicament is curiously reminiscent of an episode in *The Voyage of the Dawn Treader* (1952), in the Narnia series. Prince Caspian of Narnia and three human children, in their ship, the *Dawn Treader*, come upon a dark island where they rescue a man who is frightened out of his wits because this is the island where dreams come true, and the dreams that are coming true are nightmares. The ship stays just long enough near the island for the dreams of the ship's company to start coming true, and then the voyagers escape, with the help of Aslan, C. S. Lewis's Christ-figure.

Fortunately, George Orr's capacity for effective dreaming is not as efficient as that. Only some of his dreams come true, and they do not come true as nightmares. Although the reality they bring about is not particularly wonderful, they are definitely wish-fulfillment dreams. When George Orr wants something badly enough, he dreams that it has happened, and reality changes, not only for himself, but for everybody around him. Initially, he is the only one who has any memory of the previous reality, but later, certain people who are present at the moment of his dreaming are able to retain the memory.

Because he is a singularly modest man, the reality Orr brings about is radically different from the previous reality in only one particular—the wished-for element that he has brought into being through his dream. Any other changes occur as a necessary consequence of that one change. At the beginning of *The Lathe of Heaven*, Orr manages to survive a disastrous atomic explosion. He somehow goes to sleep, amid the wreckage of Portland, and wakes up in a tiny room in a crowded condominium, where he is suffering from the effects of taking barbiturates and amphetamines for a week in an effort to suppress his dreaming. After having dreamed away an atomic explosion, a less modest man would have been pleased with his achievement, and would probably have welcomed new dreams. But George Orr, while ordinary in some ways, is exceptional in others.

Quite apart from his extraordinary powers, he is, as critic

Douglas Barbour points out in a short but illuminating article, a Taoist sage, and he is convinced that changing the order of things is wrong. If he were supposed to perish in an atomic explosion, then he should have, accepting death when it came, instead of struggling for a life to which he is not entitled. Part of the new reality into which he has dreamed himself is a psychiatrist whom Orr is obliged to consult when his use of drugs turns out so badly, and he goes to his psychiatrist hoping to be cured of his effective dreaming.

However, in dreaming himself into this new reality, Orr has not dreamed up the right psychiatrist. Presumably it took all his strength to dream away the atomic explosion, and he had neither the power nor the will to invent a suitable psychiatrist to help him stop dreaming. After all, he has done nothing to change overpopulation or pollution, or to increase the available food supply, so there is no reason why he should set about changing psychiatrists, most of whom are decent men doing a difficult job. Unfortunately, when the psychiatrist to whom he is sent, Dr. William Haber, has proof that Orr really can change reality with his dreams, the doctor sets about using him to "improve" the world.

Their situation starts fairly mildly, with a normal doctor-patient relationship. George Orr is quite frank with Dr. Haber. He tells him that his first really effective dream had come at the age of seventeen, when he had dreamed that his aunt, who was trying to seduce him, was dead. Haber thinks that Orr is schizophrenic, and hypnotizes him into having an effective dream about a horse, in order to prove to him that it is safe for him to dream. As a result, the photograph of Mount Hood on the wall of the doctor's office changes to a photograph of a horse. At Orr's next visit, Haber makes him change the picture into a photograph of Mount Hood again. Then he makes him stop the rain.

After that, the scene switches to the office of the civil rights lawyer, Heather Lelache, who is mulatto and very conscious of her color. (Le Guin has shown us many black,

white, and brown people in her previous novels, but Heather
Lelache is the first of her characters to feel any self-con-
sciousness about color.) Orr consults Lelache about finding
some way of stopping Haber from changing reality through
his dreams. He mentions that the Augmentor, the machine
to which Haber hooks him up to put him into the dream
state as fast as possible, is experimental, and she agrees to
come to his next session as an ACLU observer. At that
session, Haber tells Orr to dream that he is no longer
bothered by overpopulation, and Orr dreams of a cancer
plague that kills six billion people. This time both Haber
and Lelache are conscious of the change. Haber realizes that
he has real power to change the world through Orr, and
Orr realizes that he cannot get away from Haber. He could
dream that Haber was dead, like his aunt and the six billion
people who died of the cancer plague, but he seems to be
clinging doggedly to his determination not to do any dreaming on his own initiative. Besides, such a terminal wish would
put an end not only to Haber but to the story as well.

Haber gets himself made head of a Dream Research
Institute through one of Orr's dreams, and then suggests
that Orr dream of peace on earth. Orr's subconscious balks
at this, and he dreams of a war in space against invading
Aliens that unites the countries of the world. Then, in horror
at what he has done, he flees to his cabin in the woods and
tries not to sleep. Heather Lelache finds him there and
hypnotizes him into dreaming that Haber is honest and
benevolent and that the Aliens are off the moon. The next
morning, the Aliens are on Earth, and the United States Air
Force is bombing everything in sight in the hope of killing
them!

Orr and Heather Lelache return to Haber, who is just as
manipulative as ever, but more honest about what he is
doing. He gets Orr to dream of peace with the Aliens. Then
he tells Orr to get rid of racism, and Orr turns everyone
gray, losing Heather Lelache in the process. After that, there
are citizen's arrests of people suffering from malignant

diseases, schizophrenia has been almost entirely eliminated by a new method of upbringing, Portland is the capital of the world, and Haber is running things from an enormous building in the center of town. But he plans to run things even better once he has learned from his analysis of Orr's brain waves how to dream effectively.

With help from an Alien, Orr dreams back Heather, who is now his wife. Then Haber instructs Orr to have an effective dream that he has stopped dreaming effectively. This works, and Haber hooks himself up to the Augmentor at the first opportunity. Orr struggles through the dissolving world that is the result of Haber's nightmare and turns the Augmentor off. Haber is now incurably insane, and Orr is free. He gets a job he likes working for an Alien, and at the end of the book he meets up once more with Heather Lelache, whom he had lost during Haber's nightmare.

Not only is Orr's power of effective dreaming magical, but it is also possible to see fairy-tale elements at work in the plot. The theme of a selfish, greedy person who uses an unsuspecting person to obtain power and riches, only to suffer for it, while the unsuspecting person comes off best, is fairly common in fairy tales. One thinks for example of Aladdin, who is sent down into an underground cavern by a wicked magician to fetch a magic lamp that the magician wants for himself, but which Aladdin ends up keeping, gaining great wealth and happiness for himself with the aid of the genie in the lamp. There is a similar situation in Hans Christian Andersen's story "The Tinder Box"; a witch sends a soldier into an underground place to fetch her a tinder box, which he decides to keep. Both Aladdin and the soldier end up rich and powerful kings, with princesses as their brides.

Another parallel is the Grimms' fairy tale, "The Pink," which tells the story of a prince who has the power of wishing and who is kidnapped as a child by a wicked old cook, who makes him wish things for him. Finally the young prince realizes the cook's wickedness and turns him into a poodle that is forced to eat hot coals until flames come out of its mouth. Again, the prince ends up as a king with a beautiful bride, just as George Orr ends up, more modestly, with a job that suits him and the company of the woman he loves, freed from the power he never wanted and the tyrant who was using him.

As far as Haber is concerned, however, an even closer parallel is the Grimms' fairy tale, "The Fisherman and His Wife." In this story, a fisherman catches a magic fish, which, in return for being spared, grants all his wishes. The fisherman wishes for nothing for himself, but his wife sends him back to ask for one wish after another. First she wants a cottage, then a castle, then she wants to be king, then emperor, then pope, and finally she wants to command the sun and the moon. She gets all her wishes but the last, although with every wish the weather gets worse and the sea rougher, as a sign of the fish's displeasure. When she asks to command the sun and the moon, the fish puts the two of them back in the wretched hovel in which they had been living at the beginning of the story. Of course, worse happens to Haber than that, but there is the same feeling of the punishment that attends presumption. One could speak of hubris, but there is no need to go as far as to Greek tragedy for examples.

One might well ask, with all these fairy-tale elements visible in *The Lathe of Heaven*, how Le Guin can consider that she had separated her pure fantasy vein from her science-fiction vein by the time she wrote it, and how it can be said that she shows more realism in this work than in the preceding ones. *The Lathe of Heaven*, once one has swallowed the idea that dreams can come true, does come across as a realistic work. One reason is that all the problems Haber is attempting to solve through Orr are only too much with us. Another reason is that Le Guin uses scientific terminology freely in this novel for the first time. Also contributing to the realism is the skillfulness of the characterization. Told sometimes from the point of view of Orr, sometimes from the point of view of Heather Lelache, and sometimes from the point of view of Haber, the narrative is carried along and rendered credible by the interaction of their personalities. Yet another factor is that Le Guin has borrowed certain techniques from Philip K. Dick, who specializes in describing "ordinary" people with extraordinary abilities.

Let us start with the scientific terminology; Le Guin is extremely precise in her treatment of dreams. When Haber sees Orr for the first time, he explains that there are four mental states: waking, trance, s-sleep (that is, nondreaming or almost nondreaming sleep) and the d-state (that is, the state of vivid, emotion-laden dreaming, which is evidenced by the rapid movement of the sleeper's eyes—REM). With the aid of his Augmentor, Haber proposes to move Orr from hypnotic trance to the s-state and then, as rapidly as possible, into the d-state. Normally, the d-state is entered only four or five times a night, for a quarter of an hour at a time, but the Augmentor is used to stimulate the brain so that first s-sleep and then the d-state are entered very quickly. Once Haber has put his patient into trance, he watches the pattern of his brain waves on the EEG—electroencephalograph. First alpha waves appear, then sleep spindles, then the delta rhythm of the d-state, and the theta rhythm from the hippocampus. When Haber tries to get the rhythm of Orr's effective dreaming in order to feed the pattern into his Augmentor so that he can receive the stimulus himself, he looks for an omega rhythm, but instead finds that Orr is simply using all the usual rhythms in a pattern of unusual power and complexity.

Le Guin has said that since she writes mainly social science fiction, she has to read psychology and biology, and that *The Lathe of Heaven* grew out of her reading about the dream research that had been coming out in the mid- and late-sixties. She had read it simply because she found it fascinating, without any idea that a novel would result. It is worth noting that she had no criticism to make of the

morality of dream researchers when she invented Haber,
but was rather launching a small attack on behaviorism.

For those who are interested in following up on Le Guin's
research, she mentions in her Afterword to "The Word for
World Is Forest" in *Again, Dangerous Visions*, that the dream
researchers she had been reading in particular were Hadfield
and Dement. In his *Dreams and Nightmares* (1954), J. A.
Hadfield, a psychologist, discusses Freud's, Adler's, and
Jung's theories on dreams. He then departs from the sexual,
power-oriented, and archetypal interpretations of dreams to
argue in favor of what he calls the "biological" interpretation.
He believes that what the dreamer is doing is attempting to
solve personal problems, which may be of any kind. The
dreams Hadfield analyzes are all real, and his interpretations
of them are very convincing. It is possible that Le Guin used
his technique of dream interpretation to construct dreams
for her characters; certainly, the dreams she describes, from
The Tombs of Atuan to *The Dispossessed*, are very lifelike. In
their irrationality they read like authentic dreams, but they
are sufficiently clear to be interpreted along Hadfield's lines,
whether or not the reader has heard of Hadfield.

The second dream researcher mentioned by Le Guin,
William C. Dement, is particularly interested in the physi-
ology of sleep and dreams. Le Guin may have obtained
much of the technical terminology she uses in *The Lathe of
Heaven* from him. Dement has published several papers on
sleep and dreams in mental illness. Like Hadfield, he is
concerned with the way the mind uses sleep and dreams to
remain healthy and sane. His *Some Must Watch While Some
Must Sleep* (1972), which appeared too late to have influenced
The Lathe of Heaven, can be used as a guide to his research.

The realistically rendered personalities of the characters
also lend credibility to *The Lathe of Heaven*. The contrast
between Haber and Orr is established from the beginning.
In their first session, when Orr says he doesn't want to
change things, Haber asks, "Why?" Soon Haber recognizes
that Orr is so passive that he could easily be dominated. And

Haber isn't one to waste time on means; he is interested only in the desired end. The relationship of exploiter-exploited that is about to develop is quite clear. In their second session, Haber reveals that he likes to have daydreams of saving the world, whereas the only thing Orr daydreams about is a cabin in the woods (which Haber allows him to obtain through an effective dream). When Heather Lelache joins Orr at that cabin, she asks him why he didn't dream of something less modest, but he says it is all he ever wanted.

Haber is convinced that he knows what he is doing, and that he is the custodian of a morality that consists of doing good to others. "Orr had a tendency to assume that people knew what they were doing, perhaps because he generally assumed that he did not." Haber is full of ideas and projects. Orr feels his way slowly, "never skating over the clear, hard ice of logic, nor soaring on the slip-streams of imagination, but slogging, plodding along on the heavy ground of existence." (One thinks here of the passage from the *Tao Te Ching* about being inept and outlandish, which Falk quotes to the old Listener in the forest.) Haber thinks he has a right to change things; Orr does not. With all his ideas about doing good, Haber would be willing to use violence on Heather Lelache to keep her from interfering with his project. Orr feels a moral responsibility even for his dreams, which he cannot control. Haber is convinced that "a mystery is merely a problem we haven't solved yet." Orr is content to go along with mysteries such as the nature of the aliens he dreams into being, simply accepting what comes. Haber is a man of action. Orr wants to act only when he has lost the sureness of foot that kept him doing "what seemed to want doing, the next thing to be done, without asking questions, without forcing himself, without worrying about it." (Here we think of Ogion, and of Rolery's *wu wei*.)

As has already been mentioned, Orr is a Taoist sage. Haber asks him, sneeringly, if he has ever studied the Eastern mysticisms, but he has not. His Taoism is not learned but instinctive. Heather Lelache, beneath her surface ag-

gressiveness, is another of the same sort. Le Guin says of
her:

> A person who believes, as she did, that things fit: that there is
> a whole of which one is a part, and that in being a part one is
> whole: such a person has no desire, at any time, to play God.
> Only those who have denied their being yearn to play at it.

Because of this, she recognizes the strength of Orr. She sees
him as being "like a block of wood not carved," which is an
allusion to the *Tao Te Ching*. One of the references to the
uncarved block runs as follows:

> Know honor
> Yet keep humility.
> Be the valley of the universe!
> Being the valley of the universe,
> Ever true and resourceful,
> Return to the state of the uncarved block.

Going on, Heather sees Orr as:

> The infinite possibility, the unlimited and unqualified whole-
> ness of being of the uncommitted, the nonacting, the uncarved:
> the being who, being nothing but himself, is everything.

In his penultimate session with Haber, Orr learns that
the personality tests taken on him show that he is "the man
in the middle of the graph." One of Haber's colleagues has
said that that means Orr has achieved "a peculiar state of
poise, of self-harmony." But for Haber it simply means that
Orr cancels himself out. After this comment, Haber hooks
Orr up to the Augmentor in a waking state, and an Alien
appears to Orr in a vision, offering help. After this vision,
Orr has a great sense of well-being.

> And, quiet as a thief in the night, a sense of well-being came
> into him, a certainty that things were all right and that he was
> in the middle of things. Self is universe. He would not be
> allowed to be isolated, to be stranded. He was back where he
> belonged. He felt an equanimity, a perfect certainty as to where

he was and where everything else was. This feeling did not come to him as blissful or mystical, but simply as normal.

The Alien has restored him to his normal mode of being, perfectly at peace with himself, and it is through two other Aliens that he is reunited, twice, with Heather Lelache. So, in his passive way, which Haber despises, Orr has dreamed himself effective allies for his natural Taoism.

The epigraphs to the chapters of *The Lathe of Heaven*, many of which are quotations from Lao Tse and from his later follower, Chuang Tse, drive the point home, and it is from one of these quotations that the title of the novel is derived. In Le Guin's version, the passage, from the twenty-third chapter of Chuang Tse's writings, runs as follows:

> Those whom heaven helps we call the sons of heaven. They do not learn this by learning. They do not work it by working. They do not reason it by using reason. To let understanding stop at what cannot be understood is a high attainment. Those who cannot do it will be destroyed on the lathe of heaven.

The contrast between Orr and Haber could not be clearer than it is in this quotation. Haber is indeed destroyed, while Orr is helped by heaven. Another epigraph, from the eighteenth chapter of the *Tao Te Ching*, "When the Great Way is lost, we get benevolence and righteousness," sums up very neatly the hollowness of all Haber's attempts to do good and the failure to which they are destined.

Other quotations from Chuang Tse concern Orr's dreams. The epigraph that heads the first chapter says that we are all dreams. This seems to reinforce the idea that everything that happens in *The Lathe of Heaven*, including the continued existence of the characters, is due to Orr's dreams. Not just the results of Haber's commands come from Orr's dreams, but the whole sequence of events from the beginning has been dreamed by Orr. Haber, Heather Lelache, and Orr himself are all dreams.

The epigraph to chapter two, "The portal of God is non-existence," introduces a discussion between Haber and Orr

about the reality of dreams. It appears to mean that everything that exists came out of nothing. In the same manner,
things that did not previously exist are called into existence
by Orr's dreams. The quotation at the head of chapter nine,
"Those who dream of feasting wake to lamentation," fits
Haber's decision to do his own dreaming and dispense with
Orr. He dreams of feasting, in the sense that he looks
forward to doing great things, but he wakes to lamentation.
As the epigraph to chapter eight, a quotation from Lao Tse,
puts it, "Heaven and earth are not humane." There is a
ruthlessness to the natural order of things that Haber fails
to reckon with. He is ignorant, and he will suffer for his
ignorance.

It is not as if he had not been warned. Orr tells him, at
their last interview, that he should consult the Aliens before
he tries his own dreaming. The Aliens belong to dream time,
and they know that the kind of dreaming Haber plans to do
has to be kept going in the right direction. Orr says:

> Everything dreams. The play of form, of being, is the dreaming
> of substance. Rocks have their dreams, and the earth changes. . . .
> But when the mind becomes conscious, when the rate of
> evolution speeds up, then you have to be careful. Careful of
> the world. You must learn the way. You must learn the skills,
> the art, the limits. A conscious mind must be part of the whole,
> intentionally and carefully—as the rock is part of the whole
> unconsciously.

In fact, Haber had already received a word of advice from
an Alien, in the midst of the Aldebaranian invasion. It had
said, "Do not do to others what you wish others not to do to
you," thereby restating Confucius's version of the Golden
Rule. But Haber failed to realize the aptness of this remark,
just as he fails to realize that Orr knows what he is talking
about.

Orr's gentleness and apparent weakness are deceptive.
Like Philip K. Dick's characters, he combines apparent
ordinariness with extraordinary talents. As Le Guin says of

Dick:

> His characters are ordinary—extraordinarily ordinary—the
> inept small-businessman, the ambitious organization girl, the
> minor craftsman or repairman, etc. That some of them have
> odd talents such as precognition is common: they're just
> ordinary neurotic precognitive slobs.

Neurotic they may be, or even psychotic, but, as Le Guin
also points out, they are capable of true goodness. Orr too
is a truly good man, kind, patient and true to what he knows
to be right. As critic Ian Watson points out, Orr's dogged
journey to reach the Augmentor and switch it off, during
Haber's nightmare, is very like Joe Chip's struggle, in Dick's
Ubik, to climb upstairs to his hotel bedroom while a malignant
force is draining him of energy. Dick's people, like Orr,
remain true to themselves no matter how bizarre things may
become. They are not always rewarded for it, but sometimes
they win through. The Christian cast of mind that Le Guin
sees in Dick's writing and her own Taoism are in accord
here. But Dick himself is something of a Taoist.

The television film of *The Lathe of Heaven*, produced and
directed by David Loxton and Fred Barzyk and shown on
Public Service Television early in 1980, is full of interesting
visual effects, but fails to do justice to the Taoism of the
novel. Orr too often appears rebellious, he protests too
much; and the Aliens, with their wise sayings, are hard to
hear. There are also a couple of needless changes to the
plot. Haber starts being honest with Orr before he is dreamed
into it, and Heather Lelache becomes Orr's wife after he is
cured of effective dreaming, instead of before. But Le Guin,
in an article she wrote on the film, seems happy enough
with it.

Her next work, *The Word for World Is Forest*, which won
a Hugo Award for the best novella of the year, reverts to the
Hainish cycle. As we have seen in all the science-fiction
novels Le Guin wrote before *The Lathe of Heaven*, there are

various unobtrusive references to the humanoid aliens called Hainish and Cetians. In *The Lathe of Heaven*, the Aliens have nothing to do with either race, but come from Aldebaran and wear protective suits that make them look like turtles. In *The Word for World Is Forest*, we actually see a Hainishman and a Cetian, and receive the news of the founding of the League of All Worlds and the invention of the ansible.

There are no direct references to Taoism in this novel, but there is a great deal of angry protest about the destruction of an ecology. The concern with maintaining the natural balance that is central both to the Earthsea trilogy and to *The Lathe of Heaven*, is directed here as anger at human greed, selfishness, stupidity, which conspire to upset that balance. There is also much interesting speculation about dreaming—not effective dreaming, this time, but waking dreaming, consciously controlled in order to maintain mental balance and solve problems.

Men from Earth have been on the planet Athshe for four years. The planet is covered with trees, and the inhabitants, who are human, do not look human to the Earth men, because they are one meter high and covered with green fur. If we discount the Aldebaranian Aliens, this is the farthest Le Guin has gone in establishing differences of appearance between Homo sapiens and the inhabitants of other planets. Even the Shing, who were supposed to be totally alien, at least looked human.

Earth has been reduced to a cement desert by human unconcern for ecology; and wood, which is now unobtainable on Earth, has become more precious than gold. Soldiers from Earth are cutting down the forests of Athshe and sawing the trees into planks that are shipped back to Earth over a journey of twenty-seven light-years. Farmers are supposed to come later and cultivate the land. But with typical disregard for ecology, the Earth men have already reduced one island to a desert by overlogging it, so that there is no vegetation left to keep the soil from eroding into the sea. And wherever they can be caught, the Athsheans are enslaved and forced to work for the Earth men on the destruction of their world. This is a far cry from *Planet of Exile*, where the descendants of men from Earth had some reason to consider their civilization superior to that of the native population.

An outstanding example of the brutal and stupid mentality that Le Guin subjects to her contempt is Captain Don Davidson. He is a handsome, muscular, well-coordinated, virile, brave, patriotic man—just the type of man to figure as a starship captain in the kind of science fiction to which Le Guin took a dislike in her late teens. He has no qualms about rape or murder—they make him feel more virile— and he totally despises the Athsheans, whom he calls "creechies" (for "creatures"), and looks forward to seeing them wiped out so that the whole planet can be taken over by men. We see the story sometimes from his point of view, sometimes from that of Raj Lyubov, an ethnologist or "hilfer," who has a great deal of respect for the Athsheans, and sometimes from the point of view of an Athshean, Selver, whose wife Davidson has killed by raping her. Lyubov and Selver are friends, and they both hate Davidson.

When the story starts, Davidson sets off for an afternoon with some prostitutes (called "Recreation Staff"), who have been supplied to the soldiers on Athshe. In a parody of the actual conditions of the American soldiers in Vietnam, Le Guin shows the soldiers from Earth supplied with prostitutes and drugs by their government and encouraged to engage in homosexuality—anything to keep the boys happy! And Davidson is happy. But when he gets back to his base, Smith Camp, he finds that it has been burned and the men killed. He does not at first think of an attack from the Athsheans, because they have been reported to be nonaggressive and have never been known to kill anyone. But then three Athsheans appear, and one of them, Selver, tells Davidson that he and some other Athsheans destroyed the camp. Then he knocks Davidson down and sings over him.

In the following chapter, we learn from Lyubov that that

was Selver's way of establishing dominance over Davidson. The Athsheans are not born nonaggressive, but they have established nonmurderous patterns of conflict and dominance as part of their culture. Lyubov, who has studied them closely, with Selver's help, had thought that nothing could make them change their ways. But Selver's anger and grief over what had happened to his wife have made him wish to kill. In chapter three we see him being hailed as a god by his fellow Athsheans because he has brought a new way of being into realization, and that is what a god does in their culture.

At Centralville, the headquarters of the Earth men, there is an official inquiry, over which a Hainishman and a Cetian, as official emissaries of the newly created League of All Worlds, preside. They are introduced as Mr. Or and Mr. Lepennon. Lepennon is a tall, white-skinned, handsome Hainishman, whom Davidson considers effeminate. Or is a stocky, dour Cetian, hairy, and with dark gray skin. When the inquiry begins they are ignorant of the way the Athsheans have been treated, but Lyubov gradually enlightens them. Lepennon, who seems to be the more civilized and humanitarian of the two aliens, is deeply moved to hear that the Athsheans have an effective barrier against killing other humans, and is equally shocked to hear that they have been enslaved. Or is more concerned with the logic of the situation, although he becomes quite sour upon realizing that the Terran colonists have not thought things through.

The two aliens donate an ansible, a recent Cetian invention, to the colony, and new orders are received over the ansible to leave the Athsheans alone. Colonel Dongh, who is at the head of the colony, determines to obey orders. This decision has come too late to save the colonists. Selver, the Athshean who has learned to kill, is already rousing his people. It is doubtful that the Athsheans would have refrained from attacking the colonists even if they had been left alone, but Davidson makes sure that they are *not* left alone. He sets out on private reprisals, setting fire to the forest and to the Athsheans. (The allusion to defoliation and the use of napalm in Vietnam is obvious.) Centralville is invaded by the Athsheans in retaliation. They kill all the women, to keep them from breeding, and many of the men are also killed. Among those who die is Lyubov, who could have warned his superior officers that the Athsheans were in an ugly mood, but did not, because that would have meant implicating Selver, whom he considers a friend.

The Athsheans round up the survivors and proceed to deal with them. But Davidson, who is in a distant camp, gets the idea that he is going to save the planet for mankind single-handedly. He is insane, and getting crazier all the time. He continues to attack the Athsheans, in defiance of orders, until they retaliate and his camp is totally destroyed. As the sole survivor, he is captured by the Athsheans and allowed to live because he adopts the position that is used by the Athsheans when they ask for life. Instead of being put to death, he is isolated on Dump Island, the island that had been destroyed by the loggers.

At the end of the novella, the starship with the Hainishman and Cetian returns and the Earth men are taken home. Selver is told by Lepennon that there will be no further attempt to colonize his planet, and the only men to come to Athshe in the future will be men like Lyubov, who will study it without trying to influence the local culture. So Selver has won a great victory, but at the cost of teaching his once peaceful people how to kill. And the lesson, once learned, will not be forgotten.

In her afterword to "The Word for World Is Forest," in *Again, Dangerous Visions*, Volume I, Le Guin says that writing this novella was easy but disagreeable, "like taking dictation from a boss with ulcers." She wanted to write about the forest and the dream, but found herself instead forced "to talk about the destruction of ecological balance and the rejection of emotional balance." Then, in her introduction to the 1977 edition of *The Word for World Is Forest*, she says that she had been participating in nonviolent demonstrations, "first against atomic bomb testing, then against the

pursuance of the war in Viet Nam," all through the sixties.
She wrote *The Word for World Is Forest* in the winter of 1968,
when she was in London and did not have demonstrating as
an outlet.

> And 1968 was a bitter year for those who opposed the war.
> The lies and hypocricies redoubled; so did the killing. More-
> over, it was becoming clear that the ethic which approved the
> defoliation of forests and grainlands and the murder of non-
> combatants in the name of "peace" was only a corollary of the
> ethic which permits the despoliation of natural resources for
> private profit or the GNP, and the murder of the creatures of
> earth in the name of "man." The victory of the ethic of
> exploitation, in all societies, seemed as inevitable as it was
> disastrous.

However, Le Guin does manage to say something about
the uses of the dream in this novella. The Athsheans sleep
very little but dream a great deal. Those who are best at it,
the Great Dreamers, can shape their dreams at will. Certain
men are Great Dreamers, while other men hunt and fish,
and the women also hunt and look after administrative
matters. The Great Dreamers tell the headwomen what they
have understood from their dreams, and the headwomen
act on it.

A few years after Le Guin published *The Word for World
Is Forest*, she met Dr. Charles Tart, who asked her if she had
modeled the Athsheans on the Senoi people of Malaysia,
who are described in his book, *Altered States of Consciousness*
(1969). She had never heard of them, and Dr. Tart pro-
ceeded to explain that the Senoi are extremely adept at
interpreting and controlling their dreams. Each morning in
a Senoi household begins with a kind of dream clinic, in
which the father and elder brothers interpret the dreams of
the children, teaching them to use their dreams to solve
problems and conflicts and invent new ways of doing things.
Waking life and the dream are interdependent, and dreaming is not considered less real than waking. This control of

and insight into their dreams has a very beneficial effect on
their psyches, and the Senoi have not killed anyone for
several hundred years. In this, the Athsheans are certainly
more like the Senoi than they are like the Vietnamese, who
have been at war, off and on, for centuries.

Le Guin feels that there are many good people like the
Senoi in the world, and that maybe we will survive with their
help. She had expressed this idea in *The Lathe of Heaven*,
where she shows Heather Lelache thinking:

> Are there really people without resentment, without hate
> .... People who never go cross-grained to the universe? Who
> recognize evil, and resist evil, and yet are utterly unaffected by
> it?
>
> Of course there are. Countless, the living and the dead.
> Those who have returned in pure compassion to the wheel,
> those who follow the way that cannot be followed without
> knowing they follow it, the sharecropper's wife in Alabama and
> the lama in Tibet and the entomologist in Peru and the mill
> worker in Odessa and the greengrocer in London and the
> goatherd in Nigeria and the old, old man sharpening a stick by
> a dry streambed somewhere in Australia, and all the others.
> There is not one of us who has not known them. There are
> enough of them, enough to keep us going. Perhaps.

6

Utopia and Dystopia

fter exposing her views on the American war in Vietnam, and on those who seek the "greatest good of the greatest number" while trampling on the rights of individuals, Ursula K. Le Guin turned her attention to politics on a larger scale. In her novel *The Dispossessed: An Ambiguous Utopia*, which won Nebula, Hugo and Jupiter Awards, she sets out to describe a planet run along anarchist lines. It is a utopia, because anarchism is the political theory that Le Guin finds the most interesting. But it is an *ambiguous* utopia, partly because the anarchist society that she envisions has defects, and partly because anarchism presupposes an endless evolution that makes a static utopia impossible. It is also ambiguous because this planet is contrasted throughout the novel with a sister planet that is split into three countries run on different authoritarian lines. One is capitalist, one socialist, and the third a military dictatorship; and life on the sister planet is far from being totally evil.

Each of the planets is the other's moon, and how things look depends on where you stand. This does not mean that Le Guin does not have preferences. She is simply using the dialectical method, presenting thesis and antithesis and leaving it up to us to arrive at the synthesis. For readers who are accustomed to having a point of view expressed in rather one-sided terms, this involves Le Guin in a further ambiguity. One of her critics has said that he has assigned *The Dispossessed* to students several times, only to find that they either thought that it promoted the capitalist society, or else drew the conclusion that one man's utopia was another man's dystopia.

The anarchist planet is called Anarres, and we see both it and the sister planet Urras through the eyes of the physicist Shevek, who has been brought up as an Odonian. That means that he accepts the philosophy of the political thinker Odo, a woman who lived on Urras in the capitalist country of A-Io, a couple of centuries before. In her day, the Odonians came so close to overthrowing the capitalist system on A-Io that they were allowed, after her death, to emigrate to Anarres and set up their own colony there, to get them out of the way. At the time the story starts, the Odonian colony on Anarres has been flourishing for one hundred and fifty years, and much antagonism still exists between Urras and Anarres.

One may wonder why Urras, which has armies while Anarres has only a rather sketchy defense system, did not attack and destroy the Odonians, once they were all gathered together. In this connection, Le Guin has said in an interview:

> The obvious trouble with anarchism is neighbors. The only time it's really been tried in a modern political state is in Spain, and they had neighbors like Russia and Germany, as well as other Spaniards. It looks as if you can't do it. Your neighbors will come and mash you flat with guns and bombs.

She gets around this difficulty by making Anarres essential to the economy of Urras. In a previous age, Urras used up most of its sources of metal, and it now depends on Anarres for supplies of mercury, copper, aluminum, tin, and gold. From the point of view of Urras, Anarres is a mining colony, and so can be left alone. This is a source of humiliation to the Anarresti, but there is nothing they can do about it. Their only comfort is that the Urrasti who come to fetch the ore are confined to the spaceport, by the terms of the original settlement.

The inhabitants of both Anarres and Urras are Cetians. Anyone who comes to *The Dispossessed* from Le Guin's earlier Hainish novels will recognize the Cetians, who have been mentioned there several times, along with the Hainish. In *City of Illusions*, they are identified as the creators of Terran mathematics, and in *The Word for World is Forest*, as we have seen, a Cetian appears. But, apart from hairiness, this Cetian and the Cetians in *The Dispossessed* have little in common. For one thing, the earlier Cetian is described as iron gray, while there is nothing unusual about the later Cetians' skin coloring. For another thing, the earlier Cetian is presented with only a slight attempt at characterization and no attempt at social background. He is simply an alien *ex machina*, disapproving, from the lofty height of his moral superiority, of the base behavior of the Terrans. In contrast, the Cetians in *The Dispossessed* are lively people, vividly described, with a strong attachment to their different societies, their political views being the main point of the novel.

This discrepancy occurs in spite of the fact that the two novels are conceived as being close to one another in time, for, at the end of *The Dispossessed*, Shevek presents the equations of his General Temporal Theory to the ambassador of Terra, saying that he wants them disseminated among the known worlds, and explaining that his theory will make it possible to construct the ansible. The ambassador reacts by saying that the ansible will make a League of Worlds possible. And so the Hainish cycle has come back to its beginning.

The Dispossessed is situated early in the Hainish cycle, before the events of *Rocannon's World*, and there is still no mindspeech. Nor are the dreams in *The Dispossessed*, apart from being visibly concerned with the deepest preoccupations of the characters, in any way different from ordinary dreams. In fact, there are no marvels whatsoever in this book, apart from the marvels of Cetian courage and solidarity under difficult conditions, and, of course, the marvel of the ansible, which is presented as a perfectly possible and logical invention. In this way, *The Dispossessed* comes closer to being a "pure" science-fiction novel—if there is such a thing—than any other of Le Guin's works. Marvels have been largely eliminated; but journeys, both inner and outer, and enemies, both at home and abroad, remain.

The first chapter shows Shevek leaving Anarres for Urras, in spite of protests from those who consider him a traitor. The second chapter flashes back to his early childhood, and from then on the even-numbered chapters, up to and including chapter twelve, show his development up to the point of his departure and explain the reasons for his leaving. The odd-numbered chapters, up to and including chapter eleven, describe his stay on Urras, in the country of A-Io, and explain why he has to return to Anarres. Chapter thirteen shows him going home, in the company of a Hainishman who wants to experience anarchism, but it is left up to us to guess what kind of a reception he will get.

If we piece the chapters together to form a continuous narrative, we see Shevek growing up in the Odonian system, acquiring Odonian values, and early realizing his bent for mathematics, which leads him to physics. As a promising young physicist, he is sent to the Regional Institute in Abbenay. (Abbenay is the center for the computers through which postings are organized and is consequently the center of Anarresti planning, such as it is.) At the Regional Institute, he is under the supervision of Sabul, a physicist with a certain reputation. Sabul is an example of the way even someone brought up as an Odonian can engage in power politics, if nothing is done to stop him. Shevek finds the idea that an Odonian is playing dominance games so disgusting that at first he refuses to admit it, even to himself.

Sabul assists Shevek by getting him to study the work of Ioti physicists, who are far in advance of those on Anarres, and to correspond with them. However, this action is far from being disinterested, because Sabul proceeds to take the credit for Shevek's work, even his work on Simultaneity, which Sabul disapproves of and hinders as much as he can, since he considers that only Sequence physics is Odonian.

While at Abbenay, Shevek runs into an old friend, Bedap, and has a brief homosexual affair with him. Then he embarks on a life partnership (the Odonian equivalent of marriage) with the young woman Takver, who is a fish geneticist. On Anarres men and women are completely equal, and Takver and Shevek pursue their careers side by side until they are separated by a planet-wide crisis, a great drought followed by a famine.

Takver and Shevek find themselves doing needed work at opposite ends of the planet, and Takver takes their daughter Sadik with her. When they are reunited after four years, Shevek decides to found a Syndicate of Initiative to combat the authoritarian and bureaucratic elements that are creeping into Annaresti life. He is influenced in this action by Bedap's discontent. He is also shocked that another old friend, Tirin, has been treated as a criminal for writing a satirical play. As a result of the activities of his Syndicate, Shevek decides to go to Urras to break down the walls that exist between the two planets. Because this is a purely personal decision, he leaves his family behind.

He also needs the stimulus that he can get from the Ioti physicists, for his work in physics is considered too esoteric to be approved of on Anarres. This is not a selfish consideration for Shevek; he considers it his duty as an Odonian to develop his talents to the utmost, for the good of the community, whether or not his community sees it in that light. Gvarab, the only one of his teachers at Abbenay who understands Simultaneity, is dead, and Shevek has to go to his enemies for the help he cannot get from his friends.

On Urras, Shevek is given a warm welcome by the Ioti physicists, who have awarded him the Seo Oen prize for his work in physics, and who give him a position at the university of Ieu Eun. They also introduce him to Ainsetain's (Einstein's) Theory of Relativity, to help him work out his

General Temporal Theory. He is very happy to have found the company of intellectual equals, for he knew no one who was his equal on Anarres. However, the Ioti authorities are determined to present their way of life to him in a positive manner, so he is not allowed to spend all his time doing physics.

Shevek is taken sightseeing and treated in every way as an honored guest, but he is not allowed to go near the poor people. Urras is a beautiful and gracious planet, in contrast to arid and inhospitable Anarres, and the ecology is well maintained, so the Ioti have much that is good to show him. Shevek is approached by a representative of the socialist country, Thu, to go there, but Shevek refuses, for he feels that the Thuvians, by imposing an authoritarian government on their people, have betrayed the revolution.

However, Shevek becomes more and more uneasy as the Ioti let him know that they want his General Temporal Theory, which unites Sequency and Simultaneity, to invent faster-than-light travel and thereby assert their superiority over other worlds. He is also distressed when A-Io sends an army to put down a revolution, which had seemed to be proceeding on Odonian lines, in the third country, Benbili. He runs away from the university for a day, and ends up taking out Vea, the sister of a colleague. She is extremely provocative in appearance but objects to open talk about sex. She is an example of the type of woman who is created by Ioti ideas of female inferiority. She gives a party where Shevek, unaccustomed to alcohol, gets drunk, tries to copulate with her, ejaculates on her dress, and vomits in a plate of sandwiches. He is then taken back to the university.

The next morning, overcome with shame, he sets to work on his General Temporal Theory. He makes himself ill by working too hard. His man servant, Efor, who has kept a respectful distance up to now, unbends when he finds Shevek ill and talks freely to him about his life of poverty. Shevek, who knows the Ioti are determined to get his General Temporal Theory, is equally determined that they shall not have it. With Efor's help, he joins some revolutionaries in the poor part of Nio Esseia, the nearest city, and a few days later addresses a vast gathering of demonstrators. The demonstration is broken up by police and soldiers who shoot to kill, but Shevek is unhurt. After hiding in a cellar with a wounded man, he finally manages to get to the Terran Embassy, where he seeks asylum. It is now that he presents to the Terran ambassador the mathematical theory that will make the ansible possible, and then returns to Anarres in the company of a Hainishman, Ketho. The Hainish, we are told, are a very ancient people, moved to generosity and altruism by the guilt accumulated over their endless past. They are friendly to other races and came to the help of Earth when it was in ruins. They have tried anarchism, along with everything else, but Ketho wants to try it for himself.

This account gives no idea of the complexity of the narrative, which is richly patterned and full of metaphors that, in accordance with Le Guin's usual practice, have a solid reality as well as a symbolic value. The metaphor of the wall, for instance, runs throughout the book as Shevek keeps coming up against walls in other people's minds and in his own mind and attempts to unbuild them; and a literal description of a wall appears in the opening paragraphs of the novel. This is the wall around the Port of Anarres, which is designed to keep the Anarresti from entering the port or leaving Anarres and to keep the Urrasti, who come to pick up the metals that are mined on Anarres, from contaminating Odonian society. Looked at from one point of view, the wall encloses the rest of the world and leaves Anarres free. From the other point of view, the wall encloses Anarres in "a great prison camp, cut off from other worlds and other men, in quarantine." And the first thing we see Shevek do is come through the gap in the wall—a deeply symbolic action.

The importance of the wall is underlined in chapter two by a symbolic dream that Shevek has as a boy. His early excursions into mathematical theory have been discouraged by an unimaginative teacher, and his father, Palat, has consoled him by giving him a book of logarithms and explaining them. Shevek then dreams that a wall stretches from horizon to horizon across the road along which he is traveling. He beats on it in despair because he wants to go home. Then his father's voice says, "Look," and he sees that his father and mother are crouching at the foot of the wall, pointing at a stone that contains the primal number, which is both singular and plural. A voice says, "That is the cornerstone," and he wakes up full of joy. This dream combines both disappointment and consolation, and the wall will continue to figure in his dreams and in his thoughts thereafter.

But Le Guin, in describing the wall around the spaceport, has said that from one point of view, Anarres is a prison camp. In doing this, she has initiated another theme-metaphor—that of the prison. All children on Anarres learn in their history lessons about Odo's imprisonment in the Fort in Drio. The boy Shevek and some of his friends shut up another boy in a prison cell they have constructed, to see what it is like; but Shevek feels his self-respect so damaged by this that, after they have let the boy out, he has to vomit.

This episode looks forward both to Vea's party, in chapter seven, where disgust at the life he has been leading on Urras combines with alcohol and sexual rejection to make Shevek vomit, and to chapter three, where he sees the Fort, a grim reality that makes other buildings look like bits of colored paper. The childhood episode also looks forward to chapter nine, where Shevek thinks of his room at the university as a gracious prison cell, and he considers certainty to be a kind of prison.

The full force of the metaphor of the prison becomes apparent when one realizes that prisons are considered an obscenity on Anarres, where there is no property and there are no laws, so consequently there is, if Odonian principles are respected, no crime. (This is what makes the treatment of Tirin as a criminal particularly shocking to Shevek.) If an

Anarresti does something that really outrages his neighbors, such as raping a woman or child, the neighbors may take revenge themselves, but the offender can escape them by entering a Therapy Center.

In chapter one, the rocks that are thrown at Shevek when he makes his way to the ore freighter that is to take him to Urras relate to a basic metaphor—a rock being thrown at a tree. This theme is stated explicitly in chapter two, where the boy Shevek attempts to explain to his classmates that a rock thrown at a tree can never hit it, because at any moment it is always halfway between a given point and the tree. This is the paradox of Zeno of Elea, which Shevek has rediscovered, thereby demonstrating his mathematical genius. He is also showing that he is already grappling with the problems of movement and time, which will be extremely important for his General Temporal Theory, as we see at Vea's party, where he explains his attempt to reconcile Sequency and Simultaneity:

> It is like this, to make a foolish little picture—you are throwing a rock at a tree, and if you are a Simultanist the rock has already hit the tree, and if you are a Sequentist it never can. So which do you choose? Maybe you prefer to throw rocks without thinking about it, no choice. I prefer to make things difficult, and choose both.

But in the first chapter, the rocks do not hit Shevek, and when the doctor on the freighter asks him if he is hurt, he simply thinks, "But the rock will never hit." Then his planet, which he views on take-off, resembles a rock falling through the darkness.

Another theme that is initiated in chapter one is that of the Beggarman. When the doctor says Shevek's luggage must have been lost, Shevek says he has none, and goes on in clumsy Iotic:

> You see, I know you don't take things, as we do. In your world, on Urras, one must buy things. I come to your world, I have no money, I cannot buy, therefore I should bring. But how

much can I bring? Clothing, yes, I might bring two suits. But food? How can I bring food enough? I cannot bring, I cannot buy. If I am to be kept alive, you must give it to me. I am an Anarresti, I make the Urrasti behave like Anarresti, to give, not to sell. If you like. Of course, it is not necessary to keep me alive! I am the Beggarman, you see.

In the next chapter, Tirin, who is fascinated by the idea of Urras, dresses up in rags from the recycling bin and pretends to be the Beggarman, who seems to be an almost mythological figure on Anarres. In chapter three, Shevek again says, this time to the Ioti physicists, that he is the Beggarman. But the Ioti are only too willing to give him money, not as a gift, Shevek discovers, but to buy him. By the time he encounters a beggar in the slums of Nio Esseia and sees the reality behind the myth, he has acquired a certain sophistication, as well as a more fluent grasp of Iotic.

Yet another theme that appears in chapter one is that of wrapping on a package. Shevek's suit has been sterilized, and when he gets it back it is wrapped in paper, which is taken off and thrown away. This looks forward to chapter five, where he feels that Urras is not real to him. When he tries to grasp it, it slips out of his fingers and he is left holding "a kind of waste paper, wrappings, rubbish." Later on, in chapter seven, he tells Vea that he has only seen the outside of the city of Nio Esseia—"the wrapping of the package." In fact, he feels packaged himself. This in turn leads up to the elaborately packaged box of candy he takes Vea, the next time he sees her, and his bitter words to Keng, the Terran ambassador, in chapter eleven:

> It is a box—Urras is a box, a package, with all the beautiful wrapping of blue sky and meadows and forests and great cities. And you open the box, and what is inside it? A black cellar full of dust, and a dead man. A man whose hand was shot off because he held it out to others.

Another theme stated early in the book is that of the jewel in the navel. Rich Urrasti women display themselves at parties wearing only sandals and long skirts, revealing their breasts and a jewel in the navel. Their bodies and even their heads are smoothly shaven, and they take oil baths to make their skin softer. The Anarresti, men and women alike, remain in their naturally hairy state, and they are not given to displaying their bodies, although some of them wear jewelry. The Anarresti, while sexually permissive, are modest. In contrast, Urrasti women, while openly displaying themselves, are supposed to be inaccessible.

This contrast first appears in chapter two, where the adolescent Shevek and his friends have just watched a film about the inequity of Urras, in which rich Urrasti women were shown lying smooth and naked in the sun, with jewels in their navels, while poor children, hairy like the Anarresti, who had died of hunger seven hundred kilometers away, were cremated. The boys are disgusted, but fascinated and sexually aroused in spite of themselves. So chapter two looks forward to chapter seven, with Vea's party.

Just as themes and metaphors connect the different chapters of the novel, so there are parallel situations. For instance, there are many contrasts between the Regional Institute at Abbenay and the university of Ieu Eun. At Ieu Eun, the students are all male and are completely freed from any responsibilities that could distract them from their study. At Abbenay the classes are co-educational, and the students are liable to fall asleep in class from fatigue after manual labor. The students of Ieu Eun are proud of the fact that entrance to the university is increasingly competitive and call this democratic, but Shevek does not think much of this idea. He says, "You put another lock on the door and call it democracy." There is complete freedom for anyone who has the talent to attend the Regional Institute at Abbenay. Shevek is pleased when his Ioti students ask him, on their own initiative, to give an open course, for this is the way things are done on Anarres, but he is disappointed when he discovers that they want him to set problems and give grades.

Relationships between men and women are very different

too, Shevek discovers. This comes up in the first chapter, where the doctor attending him expresses astonishment at the equality of the sexes on Anarres, and Shevek is intrigued by the curious eroticism of the furniture and fittings on the freighter. In chapter three, two male colleagues, Saio Pae and Demaere Oiie, insist on the inferiority of women, and Shevek realizes that they feel a real animosity. "Apparently they, like the tables on the ship, contained a woman, a suppressed, silenced, bestialized woman, a fury in a cage." He finds that Oiie treats his wife much better than his opinions had led Shevek to expect, but in Oiie's sister Vea, he meets the fury in the cage.

Vea seems very sweet and winning, but she presents herself as a sex object to such an extent that Shevek thinks of Takver's term "body profiteer," a phrase she applies to "women who used their sexuality in a power struggle with men." Shevek sympathizes with Vea in her position of inferiority to men, but she will not let him say that she is an object to be bought and sold and so wishes for revenge on men, but insists that the women really run the men, although the men are not aware of it. However, she is touched by his brotherliness and apparently would like to have an affair with him if she could keep it secret. She has to think of her reputation. But he moves too fast, and so she rejects him.

There is a strong contrast between Vea's party, where conversation is stimulated by alcohol and where Vea seems pleased to be snubbed by a man for joining in an intellectual discussion, and the easy cameraderie of the nonalcoholic parties that Shevek and his young friends attend in chapters six and eight. Also, Shevek's disastrous attempt at a complete relationship with Vea comes between Takver's proposal of partnership to Shevek and the birth of Takver's first baby, which brings the two partners closer together in parenthood. What Vea does not appreciate is that the sexual permissiveness of the Anarresti has a moral basis, the refusal to treat another person as a possession.

Like Atro, the distinguished Ioti physicist who befriends

Shevek and fights for his theories, Vea believes that social life consists of struggle and mutual aggression. She even tries to persuade Shevek that his views on morality are a relic of the barbaric past and that all morality should be discarded. Atro believes that conflict and struggle result in the survival of the fittest; Vea, on the other hand, believes that Urrasti morality covers up hate with pretty words, so she attributes no positive value to it whatever. Shevek understands her problem, and pities her.

Sex is only part of life for Shevek, and, in spite of his love for Takver, it is probably less important to him than his work. He approaches his work each time in much the same way, with fallow periods of doubt and depression followed by periods of intense activity. The burst of full-time work on physics that Shevek allows himself on arriving at the Regional Institute in Abbenay, in chapter four, and which makes him ill from overwork, is paralleled by the burst of work in which he discovers his General Temporal Theory and which also ends in illness, in chapter nine. But his work on the General Temporal Theory in chapter nine also refers back to chapter two, where the boy Shevek finds consolation for his disappointment in numbers. On the first of these occasions, Le Guin tells us that he had seen the foundations of the world, and they were solid. The second time, it is the foundations of the universe that Shevek has seen. The feeling of reassurance, while widening to suit the maturity of the man, remains constant.

Yet another theme that runs throughout the novel is that of pain. In chapter two, at the party that his fellow students give for Shevek before he leaves for Abbenay, Shevek talks about pain, which he says is inescapable. Remembering a man whom he saw dying of burns after an accident, he says that brotherhood begins in shared pain. In chapter five, he lectures rich Urrasti on the pain that brings men together, and they agree without really understanding what he is talking about. Then, in chapter nine, he says the same thing to the poor Urrasti, in his speech at the demonstration, and really reaches them. Hiding in a cellar with a wounded and dying man after the demonstration, he feels the brotherhood of pain even more strongly. And in chapter ten, when he is reunited with Takver after four years of separation and suffering, he feels it too. Pain is unavoidable, even in utopia, and one must learn how to make the best use of it. The Anarresti way of finding brotherhood in pain, instead of reasons to turn against one another, is presented as preferable to the Urrasti way.

Contrasts between the Anarresti and the Urrasti ways of life appear in every paragraph, for the Urrasti have maintained their traditions, while the Anarresti have gone out of their way to be as different from the Urrasti as possible. Although Odo came from A-Io, the first settlers on Annares did not even take the Iotic language with them. Fearing that old, harmful ideas would remain in people's minds if they used the old language, the Anarresti chose to speak an invented language, Pravic. To anyone walking through their streets, even without speaking to the people, the differences between the two cultures would be immediately apparent. In chapter four, Shevek arrives in Abbenay, which is larger than any town he has previously seen, and he walks past workshops and factories with open doors and is able to see all the activity inside: "No doors were locked, few shut. There were no disguises and no advertisements. It was all there, all the work, all the life of the city, open to the eye and to the hand." In contrast, when he is taken to Saemtenevia Prospect, the elegant shopping street of Nio Esseia, in chapter five, he is horrified by the abundance of objects for sale, and even more by the fact that the people who made them are not present:

> And the strangest thing about the nightmare street was that none of the millions of things for sale were made there. They were only sold there. Where were the workshops, the factories, where were the farmers, the craftsmen, the miners, the weavers, the chemists, the carvers, the dyers, the designers, the machin-

ists, where were the hands, the people who made? Out of sight, somewhere else. Behind walls. All the people in the shops were either buyers or sellers. They had no relation to the things but that of possession.

It is appropriate at this point to go on with a discussion of the anarchism of Anarres and what it actually consists of. To do this, it is necessary to have some idea of anarchism as a political theory. In the foreword to her story "The Day Before the Revolution," Le Guin provides us with a few pointers:

> Odonianism is anarchism. Not the bomb-in-the-pocket stuff, which is terrorism, whatever name it tries to dignify itself with; not the social-Darwinist economic "libertarianism" of the far right; but anarchism, as prefigured in early Taoist thought, and expounded by Shelley and Kropotkin, Goldman and Goodman. Anarchism's principal target is the authoritarian State (capitalist or socialist); its principal moral-practical theme is cooperation (solidarity, mutual aid). It is the most idealistic, and to me the most interesting, of all political theories.

It may be necessary to explain what Shelley, Kropotkin, Goldman, and Goodman have to do with anarchism. Percy Bysshe Shelley adopted the views of William Godwin, whose *Enquiry Concerning Political Justice* (1793) denounces law and government and recommends a decentralized society in which all goods are shared. Prince Petr Alekseevich Kropotkin was imprisoned in Russia and in France for his revolutionary views and returned to Russia at the time of the Bolshevik Revolution. His *Mutual Aid: A Factor of Evolution* (1902; rev. ed., 1914) attacks T. H. Huxley's social Darwinism and maintains that the animals that survive best are the ones that help one another. Emma Goldman was imprisoned in the United States for incitement to riot and for organizing resistance to World War I. She was deported in 1919 and went to Russia, where she was disappointed by the authoritarianism of the Bolsheviks. Paul Goodman, a writer, teacher, and dramatist, is best known for his book *Growing Up Absurd* (1956), in which he expresses concern for the full and humane development of young men. In their different ways, Shelley, Goldman, and Goodman all approved of a permissive attitude to sexuality.

The prologue to George Woodcock's *Anarchism* (1962) is very useful as giving a summary of anarchism as a political theory. He starts by pointing out that all anarchists are in rebellion against authority, but not all those who are in rebellion against authority are anarchists. The aim of the anarchist is social change, and he wants order without government. This order is to come about through cooperation between free individuals, bound by the moral law and the impulse to brotherhood. George Woodcock admits that there have been some anarchist terrorists, but he considers them a temporary aberration.

Prince Petr Kropotkin and his fellow anarchist communists attacked the wage system and considered that each individual should take what he needed from the common store. The anarcho-syndicalists, who appeared in France in 1895, laid stress on the trade union as the basis for the future free society, with the general strike as its weapon. The idea of the general strike appealed to the pacifist anarchists because it was nonviolent. Most anarchists believe in living simply, without excess or luxury, but with intellectual and artistic joys. They are against voting and parliaments because they wish to speak for themselves, as individuals, without delegating their responsibility. And they are against Marxism, which is too authoritarian for them.

One can easily see the connection between these ideas and Odonianism. Anarres is run without a government, but the moral principles of brotherhood and sharing are inculcated from the earliest years. Thus we see Shevek being taught as an infant that he cannot own the patch of sunlight in which he is sitting, but must share it or give it up. As the child grows up, he is constantly taught that he must not egoize—that is, put himself forward or show off—but must share his ideas, simply and sincerely, with his classmates. When he propounds his paradox of the rock and the tree, he is reprimanded for egoizing. He is hurt, but feels that the teacher is right, because none of the other children had understood that it was intended as a joke.

There is no private property on Anarres. People live in domiciles and sleep in dormitories. Couples who need privacy for sex have double rooms in domiciles, on either a temporary or a permanent basis. Shevek's conscience is troubled when he gets a room to himself at Abbenay, even when he realizes that he can study better alone. The Anarresti eat in common dining halls, and while the food is simple—mainly vegetarian, because fish are the only animals that exist on Anarres—and there is no liquor, there is sufficient food for everyone. When the famine hits, great efforts are made to share the little food fairly.

Anything that is needed by an individual is picked up by him at a distributory. Clothes are plain and simple, and there is little dressing up, although some jewelry is worn. Because life is simple and frugal, there is no occasion for display, and the first thing Shevek notices when he sees an Urrasti for the first time is the gorgeousness of his clothes. But Shevek disapproves of Urrasti display. Excess for the Odonians is symbolized by excrement, which is poisonous if retained in the body, and, on Urras, Shevek feels that he is surrounded by excrement.

On Urras, the general assumption is mutual aggression, while the general assumption on Anarres is mutual aid. Although the Anarresti are encouraged to think in terms of work as play and are not prevented from following their natural bent towards whatever type of work appeals to them, everybody shares in the hard and dirty work. Shevek is free to become a physicist, but he is still expected to do his share of manual labor and janitorial duties.

Any type of work that cannot be done by a single individual is done by a syndicate formed for that purpose. That is why Shevek and his friends form a Syndicate of

Initiative to work against certain elements in the system that they find repressive. Forming a syndicate is the Odonian way of doing things. Even the life partnership between two people is thought of as a kind of syndicate of two, a joining together of two free individuals to carry out a project. Apparently the importance of the syndicate dates back to the times of the Odonians on Urras; the general strike that started the Odonian insurrection was begun by a syndicate of cooks and waiters.

Doing what is necessary for the community is a moral imperative. Most of the time this does not conflict with the individual's free initiative, and there is scope for all kinds of artistic and intellectual enterprise. All Anarresti children are taught the arts along with more utilitarian skills such as farming, carpentry, sewage reclamation, printing, plumbing, and road mending. The chief art of the Anarresti is theater, because of the community spirit involved and because it does not use much paper, which is in short supply. Architecture is another much practiced art, and so is music. Painting and sculpture are treated as elements of architecture and town planning, and the only paintings and sculptures we hear about are portraits of Odo. Poetry and storytelling are ephemeral, and are linked to song and dance. Apparently no one in this novel writes novels! But in times of emergency, people on Anarres willingly give up their personal initiative and accept work where they are needed, no matter how little they enjoy it.

There is much in the system on Anarres to make *The Dispossessed* reminiscent of other utopias, particularly the *Utopia* (1516) of Sir Thomas More and the *News from Nowhere* (1891) of William Morris. But there are differences as well as similarities. In both earlier books everyone works and, although there is a distinction between men's work and women's work, everything is held in common, so that no one is poor; and everyone is fed in communal dining halls. However, marriage laws are very strictly observed in Utopia, and the Utopians conduct wars, although they try to do this without involving their own people in fighting. The Anar-resti, in contrast, have abandoned marriage because of its economic basis, and, although they are capable of physical violence, they are too individualistic ever to conceive of the chain of command that is necessary to run an army.

In Nowhere marriages are made and dissolved according to private inclination, and people are generally much freer and easier-going than in Utopia, which is tightly ruled, both by various authorities and by the observant eyes of one's neighbors. As on Anarres, everyone in Nowhere is happy in his work, and this idyllic situation started with an insurrection of the workers, in the bad old days. The education in Nowhere is practical rather than academic, as on Anarres, while the Utopians, like true Renaissance humanists, learn Greek. The Utopians are as simply dressed as the Anarresti and despise jewelry. But rich clothing is common in Nowhere, for display appealed to William Morris's artistic side.

Many other utopias could be mentioned. But Le Guin has implied, in her essay, "Science Fiction and Mrs. Brown," (1977) that reading communists and anarchists was of more use to her in constructing *The Dispossessed* than studying other utopias. And the fact remains that the system on Anarres has flaws, which sets it apart from any other utopia and makes *The Dispossessed* a more serious work than many of them.

The flaws in Odonianism are due to the fact that the success of the system depends on the private and the public conscience. Some people have inadequate consciences. The physicist Sabul, as we have seen, struggles for dominance; Desar, a mathematician at the Regional Institute, fills his room with things for which he has no need; Bunub, a neighbor of Shevek and Takver, is eaten up with malice and envy; and Shevek's mother, Rulag, works against him because when she came to visit him in the hospital, Shevek rejected her for having left his father and him twenty years before.

While the private conscience may be inadequate, the public conscience is oppressive. It is public opinion that turns

Tirin into a criminal and drives him insane, even though there are no laws for him to break. And the feeling of mutual solidarity that carries the Anarresti through the drought and famine ends up greatly strengthening PDC, the posting center, because nobody refuses a posting.

The necessity for solidarity in times of crisis becomes apparent in chapter eight, when a train in which Shevek is riding has to stop for sixty hours without provisions. It is outside a town that has food, but only just enough for its own people, so that the townspeople do not offer anything to the people on the train. Solidarity and mutual aid have gone by the board. And in chapter ten, one train driver tells Shevek about another train driver who ran some people down when they were trying to take a grain truck off his train. Shevek himself was obliged to distribute food, in one of his postings, in such a way that there was not enough for some people to live. Scarcity creates solidarity up to a certain point, but beyond that point, it destroys it, and possessiveness reasserts itself, making stringent methods necessary. The difficult conditions of life on Anarres reflect the process of turning the anarchist society of the Anarresti into an authoritarian and bureaucratic society where the individual and his initiative no longer count.

Shevek's old friend Bedap maintains that because nobody with a social conscience likes to refuse a posting, PDC was turning into a bureaucracy, even before the drought. It is possible for some people with influence behind the scenes to stay in PDC for longer than the regulation four years. And once they are in, they can use the power of public opinion to exact obedience, as opposed to cooperation, and punish nonconformists with postings to hard manual labor. Shevek's Syndicate of Initiative runs into PDC head on. In chapter twelve, we see a stormy PDC meeting where some people are talking in terms of majority rule and might makes right, in spite of the fact that they claim to be upholding Odonianism against Bedap and Shevek, who want to open up Anarres to Urras, against the terms of the Settlement. It is this meeting that makes the reader understand how much Shevek wants and needs to bring his society back to a true understanding of Odonian principles. This is in accordance with the anarchist idea that the revolution never really comes to an end.

And this is why Shevek returns to Anarres, at the end of his journey, knowing that there will be many enemies to meet him, but also many friends. He is acting in accordance with the words on Odo's tombstone:

> To be whole is to be part;
> true voyage is return.

Takver knows that Shevek will always come back, no matter how far away he goes. And he returns as he left—with empty hands. He would have liked to bring a postcard of a lamb for Pilun, his younger daughter, but he does not have even that. As a true Odonian, he has no possessions and considers that the Urrasti, with their possessions, are possessed. He has nothing but his mind, his character, and his conscience.

It is a great merit of this book that, instead of being all talk and little or no character, as is common for utopias, the characterization, even of minor characters, is very vivid. The principles that Le Guin presents are expressed in little, telling touches that form an integral part of the plot, and in ordinary conversations that are not merely a pretext for spouting political theory. There is no philosophizing, as such; every word counts, and Shevek's inner journey is as exciting as his outer one.

Although there is no overt philosophizing, it is possible to find Taoism in *The Dispossessed*. Elizabeth Cummins Cogell, in her essay, "Taoist Configurations: *The Dispossessed*," points out that Taoist thought bears a certain resemblance to modern physics, and that the scientist has to have a Taoist attitude of receptivity to the universe. Moreover, the mysticism of the Taoist may become revolutionary without losing its religious dimension. She goes on to quote from the *Tao*

Te Ching Taoist condemnations of laws, which *make* crime, and the accumulation of wealth, which is robbery. Cogell also feels that the principle of mutual aid, which Le Guin found in the writings of Kropotkin, is implicit in Taoism. For this critic, Shevek exemplifies *wu wei*, and his attitude to social action also exemplifies the inevitability of change, which is a Taoist idea.

While these insights are interesting, perhaps the most striking connection between Taoism and anarchism is the taste they both show for an organic, as opposed to an imposed, order. As Le Guin says of the rather confused PDC meeting she describes in chapter twelve:

> The process, compared to a well-managed executive conference, was a slab of raw beef compared to a wiring diagram. Raw beef, however, functions better than a wiring diagram would, in its place—inside a living animal.

We have already seen her say that early Taoist thought prefigures anarchism, and, in an interview, she has said that anarchism and Taoism appeal to the same bent of mind. But she does not underline her points by quotations from Lao Tse, Chuang Tse, or even the *I Ching*. Nor does she show us in any detail any philosophy in *The Dispossessed* that is not scientific or political, although we do get a few glimpses of religion.

Religion is known on both Anarres and Urras, although there is no church on Anarres and the Urrasti think of the Anarresti as atheists. However, few Anarresti practice religion, and they seem to regard it as rather esoteric. The Urrasti have a concept of hell and damnation that the Anarresti do not share, having kept the words for hell and damnation only for swearing. Shevek tells the doctor on the freighter that religion, as the Anarresti understand it, concerns man's deepest relation with the cosmos. Judging by the conversation at Vea's party, certain Urrasti mystics have a notion of time that is close to the concept of simultaneity, and early Urrasti physics is couched in religious terms. But that is all we learn about religion in this novel. Apparently Le Guin had pretty nearly exhausted her taste for inventing religions and religious modes by the time she came to *The Dispossessed*.

Mysterious happenings, however, not strictly identifiable in terms of religion or magic or even fairy tales, occur more and more frequently in Le Guin's work after *The Dispossessed*, which seems to mark a turning point in her career. This is noticeable in "The New Atlantis" (1975), which is divided in two parts. A science-fiction part, presented in "realistic" terms, describes a thoroughly horrible future America; and a fantastic part portrays the thoughts of the people of lost Atlantis, which is rising from the depths of the ocean. However, if one considers "The New Atlantis" from a purely political point of view, it appears as an unambiguous dystopia, to match the ambiguous utopia of Anarres.

This story, which, like *The Lathe of Heaven*, is set in Portland, Oregon, describes a Gulag world, as in the works of Aleksandr I. Solzhenitsyn. The American government still talks about freedom and democracy, but there is no freedom or democracy left. Everything is regimented; food and alcohol are strictly rationed; there are laws that cripple even the most innocent initiative, such as where and how to spend one's vacation. There are prison camps known as Rehabilitation Camps, where suspects and dissidents are imprisoned. Doctors are known as Fed-Meds and are officials of the government, and people are driven insane in the federal hospitals by behavior modification and electroshock. Being unemployed involves one in endless hours with the bureaucrats. Marriage, for some mysterious reason, is illegal. The only books available are trashy best-sellers inculcating official attitudes. Files are kept on every citizen, and the government never leaves one alone.

Almost as bad as the bureaucratic regulations is the boastful advertising that still continues under conditions of scarcity and pollution. At the beginning of the story Belle, the narrator of the American section, is riding a Supersonic Deluxe Longdistance bus that runs on coal and breaks down because the driver tries to go faster than thirty miles an hour. Later she stops for a meatless hamburger at the Longhorn Inch-Thick Steak House dinerette. Even the United States government advertises itself; Belle listens to a commercial for United States government canned water (tap water is liable to give you typhoid unless you boil it) and to another commercial for the Supreme Court—"Take your legal troubles to the Nine Wise Men!" But, in spite of all the boasting and all the governing that goes on, the only thing that seems to operate really efficiently is government snooping on suspects, dissidents, and subversives.

There are constant power shortages, in spite of the nuclear plants that supply power. Rich people have solar heaters on their houses, but they do not work very well. So there is a real need for the solar-powered cell invented by Simon, Belle's mathematician husband, and his friends. Unfortunately, there is no possibility of patenting the device or letting people have it or know about it, even as a gift, because the government wants to be the source of all power. Even more to the point, Simon is not a government employee and does not have government clearance, and so he cannot publish anything except in hectograph. However, he has had a paper published in Peking, so people abroad have heard of him, which is why he is allowed out of a Federal Rehabilitation Camp when he injures his back. He gets back to Belle, near the beginning of the story. But it does not take long for first the FBI and then the police to come, and he is taken to a Federal hospital.

Until they are separated by the intervention of the authorities, Belle sticks faithfully by her (illegal) husband, getting a black-market doctor to see to his injured back, claiming unemployment in his name and playing the viola in the bathroom, where an FBI bug has been planted, to cover the conversations of Simon and his friends. At the end of the story, she sets out to walk to the hospital where

Simon has been taken, but does not really expect to get there, because America is sinking as Atlantis rises from the depths of the ocean.

Going back and forth from one point of view to another, as is common with Le Guin, the narrative switches throughout the story from America to the bottom of the ocean, where the Atlanteans, described in deeply poetic language, are gradually coming to life. They see the fish around them, then the buildings of their city and the light of the sun shining down into the water. A mysterious empathy exists between the souls of the Atlanteans and those of Belle, Simon, and their friends. When Belle is improvising on her viola, one of her friends sees the towers of Atlantis in the sunlight and Simon hears the voices of the Atlanteans. The Atlanteans also hear Belle calling.

There is a passage in the Atlantean section that runs:

> *Later, certain sounds came down to us from above, or borne along the endless levels of the darkness, and these were stranger yet, for they were music. A huge, calling, yearning music from far away in the darkness, calling not to us.* Where are you? I am here.
>
> *Not to us.*
>
> *They were the voices of the great souls, the great lives, the lonely ones, the voyagers. Calling. Not often answered.* Where are you? Where have you gone?

One of Simon's friends says that with the solar cell he could move a mountain or sink a continent. But it seems almost as though Belle's playing has the same power and that she has raised Atlantis from the ocean depths, sinking America as she does so, in her yearning for a better world. But if this is the case, she drowns herself as well as the things she despises. There is no place for the great souls in this dystopia, so there can be no hope and no mercy for it, and no one can survive. At the end of the story, the Atlanteans say, "*Where are you? We are here. Where have you gone?*" But there is no reply.

The poignancy, poetry, and despair of this brief tale are echoed in "The Diary of the Rose." This short story appeared in 1976, two years after *The Dispossessed* and one year after "The New Atlantis." It takes the form of the diary of a woman doctor in a country where liberals are considered subversive and receive "mental treatment" as in the U.S.S.R. There is no direct indication of the country intended, but it may be Orsinia, for the name Sorde appears in it, as in Le Guin's Orsinian stories.

The doctor, Rosa Sobel, has two new patients, Ana Jest and Flores Sorde. Ana Jest is a middle-aged woman suffering from depression, but Dr. Sobel considers that Ana Jest does not have much in her life to make her happy, so there is little that can be done for her. Flores Sorde is referred to the doctor as psychopathic and violent, and it takes her some time to realize that he is in the hospital for political reasons and is destined to have his mind destroyed through electro-shock. He keeps telling this to the doctor, but she regards his statements as symptomatic of his psychosis. She is young and politically naïve. Up until now she has worked only with autistic children, so Ana Jest and Flores Sorde are her first adult patients.

She analyzes her patients with a psychoscope, a machine that projects their thoughts onto a screen. All she gets at first from Ana Jest is a kind of mental sludge and a dream about a wolf that turned into a pancake. There is a ray of hope, however, when this patient produces a clear image of a child's face and starts knitting a cap for the child. But Sorde is different. At his first session he produces a perfectly visualized rose, in response to the name Rosa—hence the title of the story. The doctor is impressed, in spite of herself, by this indication of the power and clarity of his mind.

Sorde resists her for a while, deliberately thinking of things he hopes will annoy her. But she gets something from his unconscious level, despite his efforts, and continues to be impressed by his mind. She asks to go over his childhood with him, and he agrees. As they do this, she is intrigued by an imaginary companion called Dokkay whom Sorde invented as a child, to console himself for the cruelty and injustice of the world around him. Unwittingly, Rosa is growing closer to Sorde.

For a while she has the hope, once she realizes that he really is in the hospital for political reasons, of clearing him from the charge of disaffection. She recognizes that he believes in democracy when she asks him to think about it and he plays the chorus from Beethoven's Ninth Symphony in his mind. Then she switches to thinking that he has a real psychosis when he says that he would be willing to betray his nation for humanity or for a friend. But before she knows it, he has converted her to his way of thinking. She even dreams about Dokkay. But she cannot save Sorde or herself. He goes to have electroshock, and she is out in the cold

"The Diary of the Rose" is a very direct plea for freedom and democracy as real ideals, not distorted by authoritarian governments into caricatures of themselves. It is also a plea for the right of the individual to have relationships with other persons without these relationships being distorted by political considerations. In this story, as in the other material discussed in this chapter, we have seen Le Guin's dedication to her political ideals, with love of freedom and hatred of tyranny as their two poles.

7
Mainly Short Stories

"The Diary of the Rose" is only one of several short stories that Le Guin published between 1974 and 1978. Three stories that appeared before *The Dispossessed* are "The Author of the Acacia Seeds and Other Extracts from the *Journal of the Association of Therolinguistics*," "Intracom," and "Schrödinger's Cat" (all 1974). They are comic and highly entertaining. The first speculates about the possibility of studying the art forms of animals and plants. The second describes through the metaphor of the crew of a spaceship the thoughts of a young woman who has just realized she is pregnant. And the third is a takeoff on a famous "thought experiment" by the physicist Erwin Schrödinger. Suppose a cat is put in a box with a gun attached to the inside of the box. Depending on the behavior of a photon emitted inside the box, the gun may shoot the cat or it may not. Le Guin turns this demonstration of uncertainty into a lively narrative, full of unexpected twists.

The short stories she has written since *The Dispossessed* are on the whole much less exuberant. "Mazes" (1975), a horrifying little story, describes the last living moments of an alien whose culture attaches great importance to performing dances in mazes of increasing complexity. A human scientist is testing its intelligence by putting it through mazes, without in the least understanding what the alien is doing in them. He is also starving it to death by feeding it the wrong kind of food. "SQ" (1978), a grimly humorous story, tells how a psychologist with great political influence invents a test to measure levels of sanity and forces everyone in the world to take the test. More and more people are committed to mental hospitals as a result, including the psychologist himself. His secretary, who is imperturbably sane, is left to run the world, since the psychologist is no longer capable of doing it.

"SQ" is reminiscent of *The Lathe of Heaven*, while "The Eye Altering" (1976), which describes the adjustment of a colonist's vision to a new world, is reminiscent of the idea of genetic adaptation in *Planet of Exile*. "No Use to Talk to Me" (1976) depicts a conversation in a space ship that is about to crash, while "Gwilan's Harp" tells the story of a woman's life, from famous musician to wife and mother to widow. Both these stories depend much more on emotional tone than invention.

Two other stories represent a mingling of fantasy and realism. "The First Report of the Shipwrecked Foreigner to the Kadanh of Derb" (1978) is a deeply personal description of Venice in terms that make it seem at first like a fantasy. It is not unlike the descriptions of imaginary cities in Italo Calvino's *Le Città invisibili* (1972; translated as *Invisible Cities*, 1974). In contrast, a very sad short story, *The Water Is Wide* (1976), which was published as an entire book, starts realistically and then turns into complete fantasy. As *The Water Is Wide* seems to mark a new direction in Le Guin's writing, continuing the trend begun in "The New Atlantis," it will be discussed later in this chapter, together with *The Eye of the Heron* and *The Beginning Place*.

Another new departure has been in the direction of complete realism, with the only fantasy element being the private fantasies of the characters. This is the case with *Very Far Away from Anywhere Else*. *The Eye of the Heron*, in contrast, continues the tradition of *The Dispossessed* in being a science-fiction story with a political subject, although it is much slighter and also less successful than *The Dispossessed*.

Le Guin has also responded to the public's interest in her work by having collections of earlier short stories published, in *The Wind's Twelve Quarters* and *Orsinian Tales*; poems, in *Wild Angels*; and essays and talks, in *The Language of the Night*. Besides this, she has gone back to her first subject for novels, Orsinia, and published *Malafrena*. And she has published a short piece for fairly young children, *Leese Webster*.

Wild Angels is a short collection of lyrical poems that expresses the author's feelings with dignity and reserve. Between the expression and the reserve there is a conflict that is resolved by the use of symbolic landscapes, expressing feelings in visual terms, as in the works of W. H. Auden and Rainer Maria Rilke. But Le Guin is not a great poet, as she would readily admit, and the symbolic landscapes she likes to use become more effective when they are presented as real landscapes with people in them, in her more poetic prose works, such as the Earthsea trilogy and *The Left Hand of Darkness*. When she is writing about invented characters, she is much more powerful than when she is writing about herself. This seems to be because the lyrical passages in her novels and stories are set in a pattern of allusions that link up with each other to create a great richness of texture. This texture is lacking in the poems, which are not strong enough to carry the same kind of weight by themselves.

Orsinian Tales and *Malafrena* concern Orsinia, which does not exist in the real world, but which is described as if it were real, with references to real places, such as Prague, and real historical personages, institutions, and events, such as Napoleon, Metternich, and Hitler, the Austro-Hungarian Empire, and the 1956 Hungarian uprising. Some reviewers have supposed that Orsinia is actually a real country, such as Hungary or Romania, in disguise, but in fact it cannot be identified as any particular Central European country.

For those who have acquired a taste for the marvelous

and want all Le Guin's books to satisfy it, there is something a little thin about Orsinia, a little lacking in richness and density. However, this is more the case with *Orsinian Tales* than with *Malafrena*, which reads like an historical romance. *Orsinian Tales*, moving about in time, covers the history of Orsinia from 1150 to 1960. *Malafrena* is about Europe between 1820 and 1830, when reactionary governments tried to impose order and young liberals dreamed of revolution. In both books, as in so many of Le Guin's works, love, friendship, integrity and fidelity play an important role.

Very Far Away from Anywhere Else is a very short book, but a moving one. It is written for young people, about young people, and concerns the attempt of a young man of seventeen and a young woman of eighteen to achieve excellence in their chosen fields, science and music, and integrity and respect in their relationship with each other. To do this, they have to resist pressure from society, which would like them to abandon excellence, for the sake of normality, and spoil their beautiful friendship for the sake of premature sex.

Because of their very intelligence and talent and the ways in which they plan to use that intelligence and talent, they are not yet ready for a full sexual relationship. But they share each other's thoughts and feelings. The young man, Owen Griffiths, tells his friend, Natalie Field, about an imaginary country he has invented, called Thorn, where he can be free and himself. She sympathizes with this fantasy and writes some music for Thorn. She also gets him interested in the Brontës, and he finds that they too had imaginary countries. So his private fantasy, which he had come to feel too old for, is accepted by his dearest friend instead of being dismissed as immature. This is the only fantasy element in *Very Far Away from Anywhere Else*, which is a wise, tender, and loving book, written with understanding and concern. It has been named an American Library Association Notable Book for Young Adults.

The Language of the Night will already be familiar to the

reader from the quotations that have been made from it in the course of this study. Le Guin's essays and talks on fantasy and science fiction afford valuable insights into the meaning of her works and her methods of writing. In many ways, she is her own best critic.

Leese Webster tells the story of a spider in a deserted palace, who spins pictures instead of ordinary cobwebs. When her webs are discovered, they are covered with glass and placed on exhibition. Since she has to eat, she makes webs in the garden, and is delighted to see them covered every morning with dewdrops that look like the jewels in the palace throne room. This is a gentle, humorous story, which presents the problems of the creative artist in terms that children can understand.

The Wind's Twelve Quarters, which takes its title from a poem by A. E. Housman in *A Shropshire Lad* (1896), is a chronologically arranged retrospective of Le Guin's short stories, accompanied by an introduction and notes. The first story, "Semley's Necklace," was published in 1964, and the last story, "The Day Before the Revolution," was published in 1974. As we have already seen, "Semley's Necklace" was the starting point for *Rocannon's World*; and two other stories, "The Word of Unbinding" and "The Rule of Names," were starting points for the Earthsea trilogy, while "Winter's King" was the starting point for *The Left Hand of Darkness*. "The Day Before the Revolution," which is about Odo, the founder of Odonianism, was written after *The Dispossessed* (1974).

The stories in *The Wind's Twelve Quarters* may be divided into three groups: the earlier fantasies; rather surrealistic later fantasies that take place outside time, which Le Guin calls "psychomyths"; and science-fiction stories. Apart from the stories already mentioned, only one of the science-fiction stories is directly related to the Hainish cycle. It is "Vaster than Empires and More Slow." "Nine Lives" may be part of the same cycle, but it is hard to tell, because there is no mention of the Hainish. These two stories have attracted more critical attention than the others, but all the stories are accompanied by brief introductions by Le Guin herself, which makes up for any lack of attention from other critics. It also justifies discussing all the stories in this collection in some detail.

Because Le Guin has chosen to follow a roughly chronological order in her arrangement of these stories, it would seem as well to respect this in discussing them. The first story, "Semley's Necklace" we already know. The second, "April in Paris," tells of lonely people who come together and are consoled in their loneliness. An American professor is transported to fifteenth-century Paris by a spell pronounced by a poor scholar. The American knows that no one is interested in his theories on François Villon, and the medieval Frenchman has turned to black magic in despair of success in science. Once together, they share information and become fast friends. Then they summon two women from the past and the future, and at the end of the story they are in love in Paris in the spring. This pleasant tale was Le Guin's first published fantasy story.

The next story, "The Masters," her first published science-fiction story, is considerably less pleasant. It describes a world that denies science because of the harm it has caused and that severely limits the use of numbers. Only Roman numerals are used, and the Mechanics, who use measurements, are not allowed to compute. Arabic numerals are known as black numbers and are equated with black magic. Two Mechanics secretly study mathematics and are punished by a kind of inquisition. One of them is burned at the stake, and the other has his right hand crushed. The story is full of sorrow and loss and fear. But it is also full of the joy of using one's mind and sharing ideas with a kindred spirit, in spite of any danger involved. Of "The Masters," Le Guin says, "The figure of the scientist is a quite common one in my stories, and most often a rather lonely one, isolated, an adventurer, out on the edge of things."

"Darkness Box" (1963) is a fantasy about a king who has

stopped time by shutting up darkness in a box and throwing it into the sea, so that the battle between his two sons, one a rebel and the other loyal to his father, can never come to a conclusion. But the sea returns the box, the darkness escapes, and time, change, and mortality return again. This tale is full of standard fantasy elements, such as a witch, a gryphon, and a kind of never-never Middle Ages.

"The Word of Unbinding," which comes next, is Le Guin's first Earthsea story. As we have seen, it describes a wizard's attempts to escape from a sinister enemy who has returned from the dead. The wizard has to die himself in order to defeat his enemy.

"The Rule of Names," which has also been mentioned in connection with the Earthsea trilogy, concerns a very inefficient wizard, Mr. Underhill, who is attacked by another wizard, Blackbeard. Blackbeard has come in search of his family's lost treasure, for he knows that Mr. Underhill has stolen it. He uses Mr. Underhill's true name, Yevaud, to gain power over him. On hearing that name, Mr. Underhill has to reveal his true nature. But unfortunately for Blackbeard, his true nature is that of a dragon. He was an inefficient wizard because he was not really a wizard at all, but he is a very efficient dragon. This is a light-hearted story, showing Le Guin in a humorous mood.

"Winter's King," a science-fiction story, has already been mentioned. In it, Le Guin makes use of the notion that people who go on space trips return looking quite young, while the people on their home planets have aged or died. It is an idea that seems to fascinate her, for she also uses it in "Semley's Necklace" and "Vaster than Empires and More Slow."

"The Good Trip" is not, strictly speaking, a fantasy, but a fantastic tale in a realistic setting. A young man whose wife has gone insane has joined with three friends to take LSD. He has a vision of climbing Mount Hood and meeting his wife up there. Finally they can communicate. He thinks his vision is due to the drug, but then he realizes that he has not taken it. His vision was due to his faithful love for his wife and not to any external cause.

"Nine Lives" is a science-fiction story that, as Le Guin remarks, uses an actual scientific discovery—cloning—but only as a point of departure. She is more interested in the psychological implications of cloning and its use as a metaphor than she is in the science involved. In this story, there is a strong contrast between Owen Pugh, a scrawny Welshman who had to be fitted out with a second lung and have his myopia corrected before he was sent out on planetary exploration, and the ten strong and beautiful young men and women who have been cloned from the genius John Chow. Pugh has a friend, Martin, who works with him in the exploratory mission base on the planet Libra, but the two of them cannot be closer than ordinary friends, while the tenclone is completely self-sufficient.

While the tenclone is mining for uranium on Libra, an earthquake traps and kills nine of them. The one survivor, Kaph, is totally at a loss for a while in dealing with Martin and Pugh, whom he thinks of as strangers, but at last he is able to break free from his utter dependence on the other members of his clone and accept Pugh's proffered friendship. The moral of this story is that it is hard to meet a stranger, but that real love and friendship come when the barrier between strangers is crossed.

The next story, "Things," is a psychomyth. It takes place in some unknown land by the sea. In this land, people feel the end is near, and they are killing animals and destroying things in preparation for that end. The hero of the story, who is a brickmaker, has no wish to destroy his bricks and would like to leave for the islands across the sea, but he has no boat to take him there. With the help of a widow who has befriended him, he makes a causeway into the sea with his bricks. His neighbors leave him alone because they think he is just dumping the bricks into the sea. Then he and the widow, with her child, walk out along the causeway, and a boat comes to rescue them. But they have to take one last step off the causeway to reach the boat. In her note, Le Guin says that there is always that last step to be made, past the things we possess or are possessed by, past the things we build with, whether bricks or words.

"A Trip to the Head" is a psychomyth about a forest where there are no names. Two people are standing at its edge, and a fawn is walking into it, losing its name as it goes. For anyone who knows Lewis Carroll, this is a clear reference to *Through the Looking-Glass* (1872), in the third chapter of which Alice goes walking through a wood where there are no names, with her arm around a fawn. The fawn trusts her, as long as they are in the wood, because it does not know that it is a fawn and that Alice is a human child. But when they leave the wood, it bounds away. When one of the people in "A Trip to the Head" finally gives himself a name (which happens to be the wrong one), he calls himself Lewis D. Charles. This is an allusion to the pseudonym Lewis Carroll and to Lewis Carroll's real name, Charles Lutwidge Dodgson. But mixed up with the references to Lewis Carroll is a satire on Jean-Paul Sartre and his existentialist theory that you have to do in order to be. There is also an allusion to the first two lines of William Blake's poem, "The Tyger":

Tyger! Tyger! burning bright
In the forests of the night,

The whole story comes across as a commentary on the loss of the self in dreams, no matter how full of action they may be.

Literary allusions are also important in "Vaster than Empires and More Slow." This science-fiction story owes its title to Andrew Marvell's poem, "To His Coy Mistress." In her note, Le Guin quotes two lines from it:

Our vegetable love would grow
Vaster than empires and more slow.

This is the story of vegetable love—love for a vegetation that covers an entire planet, without animals or other living beings. The man who finds that love is called Osden, and he has been sent on a mission of exploration with the title of Sensor and the task of entering into empathetic contact with sentient beings on any planet his spaceship may come to. (He is an empath, not a telepath, for at this stage in the Hainish cycle news has only just come of the discovery of telepathy on Rocannon's World.)

Like Kaph in "Nine Lives," Osden finds it very difficult to reach out, in love or friendship, to another human being. But, in Osden's case, it is not because he is already living in total contact with other selves. Osden is completely alone, because his gift of empathy with all living things makes him feel what other people feel when they meet him. Because what they feel is the instinctive revulsion and fear with which we meet a stranger and which, for most people, is covered over by good manners, Osden reacts to everyone he meets with aggressive rudeness. And it does not help very much that the other members of his crew are of unsound mind. Osden hates them all, and they hate him.

There is only one person Osden has ever loved, and that is Dr. Hammergeld, who cured him, as a child, of the autism into which he had retreated to protect himself from the consequences of his empathy. But by the time the spaceship has reached its first stopping point, a world far beyond the ken of the Hainish, Dr. Hammergeld has been left two hundred and fifty years behind, and there is no one for Osden to return to.

When Osden discovers that the vegetation on this world is sentient and that the forest-mind is afraid of the newcomers, he responds to its fear with fear. But then he realizes that the forest-mind can be loved, and that it forms the only Other he can love. So he chooses to stay behind, because his love has made him whole.

Toward the end of this story, Osden says that on this planet he feels "one big green thought." This is an allusion to another poem by Andrew Marvell, "The Garden." In "The Garden," Marvell speaks of "a green thought in a green shade." He also tells of the love he feels for the garden:

> No white or red was ever seen
> So amorous as this lovely green.

Toward the end of the poem, Marvell speaks of his joy at being alone in the garden:

> Two paradises 'twere in one
> To live in Paradise alone.

Osden has opted to live in Paradise alone and is perfectly happy. This inner adventure is what gives interest and meaning to the outer adventure of the exploration of a planet. As Le Guin says, physical action has to reflect psychic action or she gets bored.

"The Stars Below" tells the story of Guennar, an astronomer whose observatory and instruments have been burned by order of the church. He escapes the burning and is taken by a friend to a silver mine, where he can hide. The mine is almost entirely worked out, and only a few old miners still work there. They befriend Guennar, who longs for the stars and looks for them underground with a kind of makeshift telescope. He actually finds what he calls a constellation under the rock, and leaves a mark there for the miners, while he disappears into the depths of the mine. The miners dig by his mark, and find a new lode of silver.

Here, as in "The Masters," Le Guin is writing about science as an idea to be cherished, in spite of opposition from authorities. But she says in her note that she was also thinking of science as a synonym for art, and that she was attempting to show what happens to the creative mind when it is driven underground. Then she quotes a passage from Carl Gustav Jung's *On the Nature of the Psyche*, which compares the stars in the heavens and nuggets of gold in the earth to the introspective intuitions that surround ego-consciousness like little luminosities. From this she concludes that perhaps her story is about a mind turning inward to itself.

"The Field of Vision" expresses an atheist's impatience with religion. For an atheist, Le Guin has spent an inordinate amount of time inventing religions and religious modes of feeling and thinking, but here she shows how annoyed she gets when religion is forced on those who have no interest in it. She makes her point in terms of a science-fiction story. A spaceship returns from the planet Psyche with three astronauts aboard, one dead, one functionally deaf and one functionally blind. It turns out that the blind one, Hughes, is blind because he sees God all the time, and the deaf one, Temski, is deaf because he hears God all the time. On Psyche, they had entered a room constructed to teach religion and were converted in spite of themselves. Temski is perfectly happy listening to God, but Hughes resents having to see God, and would sooner see the world and people. He ends up committing suicide. The story is framed by two quotations from "The World," a poem by Henry Vaughan that expresses the belief that the vision of God is reserved for the elect.

"Direction of the Road" is a fantasy about a tree beside a road, told from the point of view of the tree. Le Guin supposes that the tree is fully conscious of the way it appears to people moving along the road. In fact, the tree actually works at looming over an approaching person and dwindling behind a departing person. In a tone that is at once sad and comic, the tree describes how much more difficult life has become now that the road is full of cars and he has to loom and dwindle continually at high speeds. But what offends him most is that a motorist has died by crashing into his trunk, obliging him to take on the aspect of eternity. This story is a protest against human carelessness of life and an expression of affection for a tree—a particular tree that Ursula K. Le Guin identifies in her note.

"The Ones Who Walk Away from Omelas," which won a Hugo Award, has the subtitle, "Variations on a Theme by

William James." In her note, Le Guin explains that the central theme of the psychomyth comes from a passage in William James's "The Moral Philosopher and the Moral Life." In this work, he says that one could not accept a happiness shared with millions if the condition of that happiness were the suffering of one lonely soul. "The Ones Who Walk Away From Omelas" describes a town whose inhabitants are all perfectly happy, but know that their happiness depends on the suffering of a feeble-minded child, locked up alone in a small, dark room. Most of them stay and enjoy their happiness, but some people walk away from Omelas—where to, it is not known.

"The Day Before the Revolution" won a Nebula Award. Le Guin says it is about one of the ones who walked away from Omelas. It describes the last day in the life of Odo, and is dedicated to the memory of Paul Goodman. It is the day before the General Strike, the start of the Odonian uprising on Urras. But Odo will not live to see the revolution for which she has worked all her life, because she will have her "private stroke" before the General Strike. The story is told with deep sympathy for the plight of an old woman, and may be taken as a blow against prejudice toward the aged, about which Le Guin had already had a few words to say in *The Word for World Is Forest*, as well as a tribute to those who refuse to rest while there is still suffering in the world.

So ends *The Wind's Twelve Quarters*, moving from tender, romantic stories to what Le Guin calls "something harder, stronger and more complex." It also shows a movement from private concerns to public ones, which parallels the development in her novels from *Rocannon's World* to *The Dispossessed*. And it maintains the Taoist theme by using the yin-yang symbol as a logo throughout. But now we have to turn to some of her most recent works.

The Water Is Wide, although published as a separate book rather than as a story in a collection, is very short. It starts off with a physicist, Gideon, in a rest home after a breakdown.

He is being visited by his widowed sister, Anna, who is the only person to communicate with him. He is borne down by distress over all the dead and dying in the world, and cannot tolerate the use of physics to bring about widespread destruction. Anna asks the doctor in the rest home if it is really necessary to give him drugs. She feels that Gideon needs to grieve fully and completely, without his consciousness being dulled.

One day, Gideon and Anna walk out of the rest home and go to a lake. When they reach the lake, the fantasy element takes over, representing Gideon's madness. In the rest home he had felt dead people lying on top of him. Now he sees a vast throng of people in the lake, swimming and drowning, and he and Anna wade out together, while Gideon's dead wife and Anna's dead husband feel them approaching. At the end of the story, we see Gideon and Anna step out on a shore, but whether it is the shore of death or not is not quite clear. Le Guin calls the place they have come to "the beginning place," looking forward to a passage in *The Eye of the Heron* and the title of her 1980 novel, *The Beginning Place*.

The Eye of the Heron (1978) is a science-fiction novel that, like so many of Le Guin's works, uses shifting points of view. It tells the story of Luz Marina Falco Cooper, the daughter of Boss Luis Falco, who lives in Victoria City, on the planet Victoria, some time in the future. Luz has been brought up to recognize the power of men and expect an arranged marriage and motherhood. But she is much stronger than she thinks she is, and, from the first time we see her, she defies her father, in small ways at first and then in open rebellion. Through Luz, Le Guin continues to explore the feminist point of view, which she had started to examine in *The Left Hand of Darkness* and taken farther in *The Dispossessed*.

But, as in *The Dispossessed*, the theme of feminism is secondary to that of politics. Victoria is largely unexplored, and there are only two settlements on it, Victoria City and the town of Shantih (which means "peace" in Hindi and

Sanskrit). Victoria City was founded a hundred years previously by criminals exiled from South America, although
the citizens prefer to say that they are descended from men
who were too strong and brave to be tolerated by the
womanish people of Earth. The men of Victoria City have
a cult of violence and domination, and despise the people of
Shantih, which they call Shanty-Town. For them, the farmers
of Shantih are peasants, made to serve them by producing
the food they need.

The people of Shantih arrived on Victoria fifty-five years
previously, having been exiled from Earth for being demonstrators for peace. They cherish the memory of the Long
March that their parents had led, starting out in Moscow
and walking across Europe to Lisbon, where they had taken
ship to North America. There, in the north, they had been
promised land to build a new community. Two thousand
people were expected in Montreal, but so many people
joined the Long March, in protest against war, that ten
thousand arrived. There was not enough land for all of
them, and they were put in prison camps. Finally, two
thousand of them were sent to Victoria.

The people of Shantih have kept the memory of the
techniques of nonviolent resistance worked out by Mahatma
Gandhi and Martin Luther King. So when a difference of
opinion arises between them and the Bosses of Victoria City,
they know exactly what to do. First they have to try negotiation by existing means and institutions. Then they have to
go on to noncooperation. After that, they have to issue an
ultimatum, and if the ultimatum is not accepted, they have
to move on to civil disobedience. But at no point must they
use violence.

Since their arrival on Victoria, the people of Shantih
have not had occasion to use these techniques. But by the
time of this story, there are too many people in Shantih and
Victoria City for the farmers to feed, and the people of
Shantih want to start a new settlement in the north. But the
Bosses do not want to let them go. Instead, the Bosses plan

to establish large estates, with the Shantih people working on them and the Bosses living like little kings.

The people of Shantih, led by an older woman, Vera Adelson, and a young man, Lev Shults, organize resistance to the Bosses' plans, using the techniques of nonviolence. The Bosses, led by Luis Falco, plan to use violence against them in order to outrage them into using violence back, so that they can punish them as rebels by using them on the new estates. Luis Falco is assisted in this plan by Herman Macmilan, the young man whom he sees as his prospective son-in-law, and Herman Macmilan gets a little brigade together.

But Luz discovers the plan and goes off to warn Lev Shults, with whom, without realizing it, she is in love. Once in Shantih, she decides to stay. Luis Falco is in despair at losing her, and when a confrontation takes place between the people of Shantih and Herman Macmilan's soldiers, and Herman Macmilan starts shooting, Luis Falco kills him. But Lev is also dead, killed by Herman Macmilan, and Luz has lost her love. However, she still refuses to go back to her father; and, at her instigation, groups of people leave Shantih in secret and set out to found new settlements. Out in the wilderness they find a "beginning place."

This is a sad story, for the nonviolent techniques of the people of peace are shown to be inadequate to resist effectively the violent techniques of the Bosses. After Lev's death, there had been a physical struggle between the people of Shantih and Herman Macmilan's brigade, and the principles of nonviolence were abandoned. After that, there was nothing to do but go back to negotiation and accept compromise, or else run away. Running away is Luz's solution, and it is accepted by many of the people of Shantih. But it is a very discouraging solution for someone who has taken part in the peace movement, and *The Eye of the Heron* is far less optimistic than *The Dispossessed*.

There is another rather disconcerting aspect to *The Eye of the Heron*, for those who are accustomed to the way strange fauna and flora blend in with familiar species in the places Le Guin invents. The fauna and flora of Victoria are very different from those we know on Earth, and there is no way in which the animals can be tamed. The people of Victoria have given familiar names, such as "heron" and "coney," to the animals, but the animals called by these names have very little in common with real herons or rabbits.

The Eye of the Heron owes its title to a passage in which Lev is returning the gaze of a "heron":

> He gazed back, and for an instant was caught in that round transparent eye, as depthless as the sky clear of clouds; and the moment was round, transparent, silent, a moment at the center of all moments, the eternal present moment of the silent animal.

That gaze puts the human being in his place and points out how ephemeral and ineffective his activity must be. Lev dies young and to no avail. The animal, which is concerned with being, not doing, outlives him. And Luz has to go on without Lev, adding one exile to another, with no hope except that of beginning again.

There is something about *The Eye of the Heron* that is reminiscent of *Planet of Exile*. Like Rolery, Luz leaves her home and family for a despised stranger. And although she is more aggressive than Rolery and Lev is more idealistic than Jakob Agat, the choices Luz has to make, like Rolery's, are both limited and important. Like Rolery, Luz fights no war. She does not even fight the war of nonviolence, although she brings help, but has to stand by while the man she loves risks his life and dies. And if Jakob Agat had died and the Gaal had conquered, Rolery too might well have run away. It may even be a Taoist solution, since the early Taoists frequently lived in obscurity or even committed suicide to escape being obliged to take office, which they considered a disaster.

Unlike *The Eye of the Heron*, *The Beginning Place* is set in the present, in an American town that is depressing in its

ugliness and artificiality. The first chapter tells how Hugh
Rogers, a young checker in a supermarket, finds a marvelous
place in the woods, a place where it is always twilight and
time runs much more slowly than it does outside. He is very
glad to go there, because there he has time to think and to
be. There is a stream in the woods, and he drinks from it
and bathes in it, feeling the water is holy. He explores the
woods, rejoicing in the absence of people and cars and litter.
But then he comes across a sign that reads, "Keep Out—No
Trespassing." It has been put there by Irene, the girl we
meet in the second chapter. She has been going to the
twilight land for years, and resents anyone else coming to
what she calls "the beginning place"—the place on the very
outskirts of the enchanted land, where Hugh Rogers had
been content to stay. From then on, the story is told from
their alternating points of view, for eight chapters. The
ninth chapter shows Hugh and Irena, as she is called by
those who love her, united and back in the United States.
This chapter is told from both points of view.

In the body of the book, the story is told of how first
Irena and then Hugh come to a town in the twilight world,
where Irena has been many times before. Irena, who knows
the language, interprets for Hugh. They are told that there
is danger menacing the twilight land, and Hugh and Irena
go forth to face it, with a sword presented to them by the
Lord of the Manor. The danger takes the shape of a
thoroughly disgusting kind of dragon, white, ice-cold, and
sobbing in hunger and pain, quite different from the fiery,
wise, and beautiful dragons of Earthsea. When Hugh and
Irena first see it, the shock is too much for them, and they
run away and hide. But then they go on to the dragon's
cave, where Irena challenges it to come out, and Hugh kills
it. However, Hugh does not escape uninjured. The dragon
falls on him in its death throes, breaking one of his ribs and
cracking another. In spite of his injuries, Hugh makes
surprisingly successful love to Irena, but when they get back
to the United States, she has to take him to the hospital.

Then Hugh's mother says that she does not want him back, and the two young people prepare to share an apartment. Apparently they do not intend to return to the twilight world.

They are happy to have found one another, for they have had miserable home lives. Hugh has been living with his mother, who is out of her mind and spends most of her free time practicing spiritualism. She has depended on him for years and has successfully prevented him from attending evening courses in library science. Wanting to be a librarian is a reasonable ambition for Hugh, who, like George Orr, is a diffident and modest hero, and he longs for the peace and quiet of a library. So it is a positive relief when his mother rejects him. Irena's home situation is even worse. Her stepfather has tried to rape her, and she is afraid to tell her mother. Because of this, she cannot stay at home, but she cannot afford an apartment on her own. Each is the solution to the other's problem, on a practical as well as an emotional level.

But the union in which they end was not there at the beginning. It takes them some time to trust and love one another to the point where Hugh can say that they are married, even though no official ceremony has been performed. For a while, Irena is in love with the Master of the twilight town and Hugh is in love with Allia, the daughter of the Lord of the Manor. However, neither the Master nor Allia deserves this love. Allia sees Hugh simply as the hero who is going to kill the dragon, while the Master would have offered Irena up as a sacrifice to the dragon if he had not been too terrified to go near it.

This account invites a psychological interpretation. One possible interpretation might go as follows. Two adolescents are having a very difficult time with their families. They are held down and prevented from branching out by their mothers' need for them. To make up for this, they live more and more in a world of fantasy. This has its dangers. They could get caught in the fantasy world and stay there. If Irena

married the Master or if Hugh married Allia or else succeeded in dying for her, as he thinks of doing, there could
be no return to reality. But the two young people are
basically healthy and sane, and so their fantasy is basically
healthy, too.

There is a contrast in this respect between Hugh and his
mother. Hugh's mother is insane in her pursuit of the occult,
but Hugh's venture into a magic world is not insane. As Le
Guin presents it, he is using his creative imagination con-
structively, to find a deeper and more satisfying reality, not
to escape from reality altogether.

When the dragon appears, it is like the mother, calling
out for pity and ready to devour her children in the name
of that pity. Hugh takes the sword and kills the dragon.
And, in the real world, it is the fact that Hugh breaks with
his mother that gives the two young people their freedom.
But it is worth mentioning that Hugh does not see the
dragon as female, although Irena sees its teats. This could
mean that Hugh kills the symbol of his mother and that of
Irena's stepfather at the same time. After the death of the
dragon, Irena is no longer tempted to expose herself to the
onslaughts of her stepfather out of pity for her mother.

This is only one interpretation, and other interpretations
are possible. For instance, John Updike, who reads *The
Beginning Place* in a much more sexual way, sees the dragon
as representing "our sorry carnality," which menaces Hugh
and Irena in their passage from solitary masturbation to a
true sexual encounter. But what makes any interpretation
of this novel very difficult is that Le Guin herself has said,
in a personal letter, that she has "very little idea what it
'means.'"

The idea that Le Guin did not write this novel with a
definite message in mind is disconcerting, for her faithful
readers are used to her presenting a message or pointing a
moral in most of what she writes. But it seems that there is
no message in *The Beginning Place* except the familiar one of
the importance of love. It is true that this does come through

clearly, but in much of this novel Le Guin is playing with the contrast between the fantasy world and the real world for the sheer joy of it.

The Beginning Place is rather reminiscent of magic realism. That is a genre in which realism and fantasy are interwoven, so that the real world becomes magical. This fantastic version of reality is cultivated for its own sake, without any didacticism. It is widely used in South America, particularly by Jorge Lois Borges, a quotation from whose poem "Heráclito" is included as an epigraph to The Beginning Place. The poem, which is strange and beautiful, is about the river of time, with night and day, waking and dreaming. It seems that The Beginning Place is also about waking and dreaming, as well as about love and the lack of it. But the dreams are intended to speak directly to the unconscious of the reader, as dreams do.

In this way, this novel marks a new departure. The references to the "beginning place" that we have noticed in the last three works discussed indicate that Le Guin has been trying to reach beyond the point she has previously reached and begin again. This makes waiting for her next novel even more interesting than it usually is, and also makes any conclusion only temporary—as is always the case with a living writer. But it is noticeable that, however much Le Guin may strike out on new paths, nothing can make her abandon her affirmation of the importance of love or her longing for a place where things are fair and seemly, where nature is not spoiled.

8

Summing Up

ven if this conclusion has to be temporary, it is possible to see, on looking back over the ground covered from *Rocannon's World* to *The Beginning Place*, certain constant themes that mark these varied works of science fiction and fantasy as the product of one mind. And, since that mind is a highly civilized one, we benefit from contact with it, even as we are carried along on the journeys and gaze in wonder at the marvels with which it presents us.

To begin with, there are the outer journeys. Rocannon travels across half a world and develops great powers in the process. But as important as these great powers are the love and grief he also learns. Falk-Ramarren travels across a continent and acquires self-knowledge, running great risks to do so. Ged and Arren travel around Earthsea, also acquiring self-knowledge and learning to use power. Genly Ai and Estraven travel across the ice, learning to love one another. Shevek goes from moon to moon, growing in insight and ability and learning that to voyage truely is to return. Owen Pugh teaches friendship, on a distant planet, to a young man who had never known the need of it. Osden goes far into outer space and learns to love a forest. Luz leaves home and goes into the wilderness, learning the ways of love, freedom, and peace. And Hugh Rogers and Irena travel into a twilight world to kill a dragon and come home again, joined in love.

Then there are the purely inner journeys. Jakob Agat and Rolery each meet the Alien in love and learn a new way of being. Tenar explores the Labyrinth, which is a symbol of her own unconscious mind, and in it meets Ged, whom she learns to love and who leads her out into freedom. George Orr travels through the world of dream and experiences its many changes, although he never goes far from Portland. He too finds love. Selver also travels through the world of dream, and finds a new way of life for his people. He does not find love, because he had known love and lost it, tragically. But his friend Lyubov, after death, walks with him in his dreams. And Belle and Simon make discoveries of great power, in exploring the worlds of science and music, although they stay as close to Portland as they can. They do not need to look for love, because they have it already. That and their genius are, in fact, the only things they do have.

But it is of limited interest to make distinctions between outer journeys and inner ones, because the difference, for Le Guin, is purely a matter of form. Questions of form have their importance for such a careful artist, and one should not overlook them. But, in the end, the outer journey is also an inner one. As we have seen, physical action, for her, has to match psychic action. As a result, dreams have great importance as inner journeys in her works, not only in the novels that have dreams as a principal topic, but in many of the others as well. They form journeys within the journey.

The worlds and countries through which her people travel are places of the mind. Forests and seas abound in them. It is not accidental that these are archetypes of the unconscious. Le Guin found them in her own mind before finding them in Jung. The creatures that people these worlds and countries are also archetypal. Dragons are frequently met with, although only in the fantasy, not in the science fiction, and the other animals and plants usually have a familiarity to them that is not always due to their similarity to the fauna and flora of Earth. There are also languages spoken in these places that have a peculiar fitness to them.

Then the marvels must be considered. Mindspeech, empathy, the ansible, and the capacity for effective dreaming are all symbols for such everyday events as the capacity for minds to meet or for an individual mind to solve problems in sleep. The mind, whether dreaming or waking, is Le Guin's kingdom, and the meeting of minds in love and friendship is the glory of that kingdom. She particularly likes to show a man and a woman forming a couple. She is a feminist, but she is not opposed to men. Hence the importance of marriage in her works, even if she chooses to call it something else. She has said:

> One thing I seem to have dug up is this: the "person" I tend to write about is often not exactly, or not totally, either a man or a woman. On the superficial level, this means that there is little sexual stereotyping—the men aren't lustful and the women aren't gorgeous—and the sex itself is seen as a *relationship rather than as an act.* . . . Once I was asked what the central, constant theme of my work was, and I said spontaneously, "Marriage."

Because love and friendship require fidelity, betrayal enters into the picture. But the betrayals that take place are not often betrayals of love. Rather, they are betrayals of a larger entity for the sake of an individual or group of individuals. Although the societies they come from are very different, Estraven and Shevek are both considered traitors because they do not put their countries before their friends. And Lyubov really does betray his fellow Terrans for the sake of Selver. Political considerations, as we have seen, have grown in importance in Le Guin's work. But her politics can be summed up as hatred of oppression and love of freedom, as they affect the individual, whether she is describing feudal lords, future Americans, Orsinians, or anarchists. Her interest in ethnology has led her to imagine widely differing societies, but each is judged by the extent to which it fosters love and friendship and permits human dignity. Her stress on the individual is connected with her interest in anarchism.

As we have also seen, this attitude is also connected with Taoism, which is a central theme in her work. We should note that Le Guin is not alone in this interest. Ever since the fifties, there has been an interest in North America in Taoism, in Zen Buddhism (which is related in outlook and approach to Taoism), and in the *I Ching*. This interest has been considered by those who do not share it as manifesting a disquieting anti-intellectualism and antirationalism. But, in fact, it really represents an attempt to achieve a holistic outlook in which the reason and the emotions are no longer divided, and the solutions to problems are sought with the full wholeness of one's being. It is for seekers of this kind that Le Guin writes, because she shares their search.

Le Guin is a seeker who uses her imagination. If she returns again and again to fantasy and science fiction, it is not only because these genres are traditionally ones that make use of journeys and marvels. It is also because they offer great scope to the creative mind. Le Guin is convinced, as she explains in her essay, "Why Are Americans Afraid of Dragons?", that we must use imagination, as long as it is disciplined by art, for our minds to be fully alive and well.

She says this in defense of fantasy. But what is true of fantasy is, for her, also true of science fiction. She recognizes that they are different forms and, after her early novels, she has tried not to mix them. But, all the same, she feels that there is a similarity between them. In "A Citizen of Mondath," she says: "Those who dislike fantasy are very often equally bored or repelled by science." And, in "Do-It-Yourself Cosmology," she calls science fiction "a modern, intellectualized, extraverted form of fantasy."

Le Guin respects the scientist, taking particular interest in the mathematician, the astronomer, and the physicist, because each is as dedicated to his goal as the artist, and as lonely. But because she makes use of the "soft sciences" of biology, ethnology, and psychology, and has little use for technology, there is a close connection between her fantasy and her science fiction. The connection is too close, in fact, for them to be discussed separately. The connection is that of freedom, love, courage, and adventure, in the inner and the outer worlds.

Le Guin is a romantic, and as a romantic she values love, nature, adventure, marvels, dreams, the imagination, and the unconscious. Like the romantics, she is aware of the dark side of things and is attracted by it, even when she prefers the light. She values the individual and his or her struggle for personal liberation. And she éxpresses that struggle in a language that, while straightforward, makes use of poetic metaphor. But like the Brontës, she manages to be romantic and realistic at the same time. Her early apprenticeship to the description of people's daily lives, even if those lives were led in a country that cannot be found on any map, taught her skill in handling specific detail. She uses that skill to good effect in her fantasy and science fiction.

However, it is hardly surprising that she did not find a publisher for her first novels. Romantics are not welcome nowadays in mainstream literature. It is in fantasy and science fiction that such an unfashionable attitude can find a home, since these genres offer a great deal of liberty to the writer. Certain conventions have to be observed, but within these conventions there is scope for the widest variety of outlook, approach, and style. Because of her love of personal freedom, Ursula K. Le Guin has chosen the genre that affords the greatest freedom to her mind, for which we can well be grateful.

Notes

Chapter 1	Quote	Source
p. 2	elegance and style	Harlan Ellison, ed., *Again, Dangerous Visions*, vol. 1 (New York: Doubleday, 1972), p. 28.
p. 3	Inner Lands	Edward John Moreton Drax Plunkett Dunsany, *A Dreamer's Tales* (Freeport, New York: Books for Libraries Press, 1969), p. 1.
p. 3	my native country	Le Guin, *The Language of the Night: Essays on Fantasy and Science Fiction*, ed. and with introductions by Susan Wood (New York: Putnam), p. 26.*
p. 5	be found—discovered	Ibid., p. 49.
p. 5	of fancy artillery	Le Guin, *The Language of the Night*, p. 27.
p. 5–6	Drabble, Calvino, Dick	Le Guin, "A Response to the Le Guin Issue," *Science-Fiction Studies*, 3, 1 (March 1976): 4.
p. 7	it all done	Interview of Le Guin by Barry Barth, "Tricks, Anthropology Create New Worlds," *Portland Scribe* (May 17–23, 1975): 9.
p. 9	vain and hasty	Le Guin, *The Language of the Night*, pp. 28–29.

* For complete publisher information see acknowledgments immediately following Notes on page 159. See also Bibliography starting page 161.

p. 12	be, my country	Ibid., p. 30.
p. 12	and all that	Le Guin, Introductory note to "Vaster than Empires and More Slow," in *The Wind's Twelve Quarters* (New York: Harper & Row), p. 181.
p. 13	concrete and simple	Le Guin, "From Elfland to Poughkeepsie," in *The Language of the Night*, p. 93.

Chapter 2

p. 15	up with neither	Le Guin, *The Language of the Night: Essays on Fantasy and Science Fiction*, pp. 134–35.
p. 23	cultures and societies	Ibid., pp. 140–41.
p. 25	nor a prediction	Le Guin, "A Response to the Le Guin Issue," *Science-Fiction Studies*, 3, 1 (March 1976): 46.
p. 28	I ever wrote	Le Guin, *The Language of the Night*, p. 146.
p. 29–30	speak the truth	Ibid., p. 147.
p. 32	Mother the Way	Le Guin, *City of Illusions* (New York: Ace Books), pp. 46–47. This passage (chapter twenty of the *Tao Te Ching*) may be found, in a different translation, in Lao Tsu, *Tao Te Ching*, transl. by Gia-Fu Feng and Jane English (New York: Knopf), p. 49.
p. 33	take another journey	Le Guin, *The Language of the Night*, p. 147.
p. 35	George Edgar Slusser	George Edgar Slusser, *The Farthest Shores of Ursula K. Le Guin* (San Bernadino, Ca.: The Borgo Press, 1976), pp. 15–16.

Chapter 3

| p. 36 | older kids | Le Guin, *The Language of the Night*, p. 51. |

p. 36–37	a larger context	Ibid., p. 55.
p. 56	T. A. Shippey	T. A. Shippey, "The Magic Art and the Evolution of Words: Ursula K. Le Guin's Earthsea Trilogy," *Mosaic* 10, 2 (Winter 1977): 161.
p. 56	to the bride	A. E. Housman, The Collected Poems of A. E. Housman (New York: Holt), p. 25.

Chapter 5

p. 83	of the medium	Le Guin, *The Language of the Night*, pp. 29–30.
p. 84	Douglas Barbour	Douglas Barbour, "*The Lathe of Heaven:* Taoist Dream," *Algol* 21 (Nov. 1973): 22–24.
p. 89	Le Guin has said	Le Guin with Charles Bigelow and J. McMahon, "Science Fiction and the Future of Anarchy: Conversations with Ursula K. Le Guin," *Oregon Times* (Dec. 1974): 26.
p. 92	the uncarved block	Lao Tsu, *Tao Te Ching*, transl. by Gia-Fu Feng and Jane English, p. 65.
p. 93	lathe of heaven	This passage, and subsequent quotes attributed to Chuang Tse appear in a different form in Chuang Tzu, *The Complete Works of Chuang Tzu*, transl. by Burton Watson (New York: Columbia University Press, 1968), p. 254.
p. 95	neurotic precognitive slobs	Le Guin, *The Language of the Night*, p. 175.
p. 95	Ian Watson	Ian Watson, "Le Guin's *Lathe of Heaven* and the Role of Dick: The False Reality as Mediator," *Science-Fiction Studies* 2, 1 (March 1975): 70.

p. 95   on the film   Le Guin, *"The Lathe of*
                                  Heaven," Horizon (Jan. 1980):
                                  33–36.
p. 99   boss with ulcers   Harlan Ellison, ed., *Again,*
                                  Dangerous Visions, Vol. I (New
                                  York: Doubleday, 1972), p.
                                  108.
p. 99   of emotional balance Ibid.
p. 100   in Viet Nam   Le Guin, *The Language of the*
                                  Night, p. 151.

Chapter 6
p. 103   One of her critics   Joseph D. Olander and
                                  Martin Harry Greenberg,
                                  eds., *Ursula K. Le Guin* (New
                                  York: Taplinger Publishing
                                  Co., 1979), p. 123.
p. 103   guns and bombs   Ursula K. Le Guin with Win
                                  McCormak and Anne Mendel,
                                  "Creating Realistic Utopias:
                                  'The Obvious Trouble with
                                  Anarchism is Neighbours,'"
                                  Seven Days (April 11, 1977): 8.
p. 116   "all political   Ursula K. Le Guin, *The Wind's*
             theories"   *Twelve Quarters* (New York:
                                  Harper & Row, 1975), p. 285.
p. 122   Elizabeth   Elizabeth Cummins Cogell,
             Cummins Cogell   "Taoist Configurations: *The*
                                  Dispossessed" in Joe De Bolt,
                                  ed., *Ursula K. Le Guin: Voyager*
                                  to Inner Lands and to Outer
                                  Space (Port Washington, N.Y.,
                                  and London: Kennikat Press,
                                  1979), pp. 153–79.
p. 123   in an interview   Le Guin with Charles Bigelow
                                  and J. McMahon, "Science
                                  Fiction and the Future of
                                  Anarchy: Conversations with
                                  Ursula K. Le Guin," p. 29.

Chapter 7

p. 137	of the night	William Blake, *Poetry and Prose of William Blake*, ed. Geoffrey Keynes (London: The Nonesuch Library, 1956), p. 72.
p. 137	and more slow	Andrew Marvell, *The Complete English Poems*, ed. Elizabeth Story Donno (New York: St. Martin's Press, 1974), p. 51.
p. 139	a green shade	Ibid., p. 101.
p. 139	this lovely green	Ibid., p. 100.
p. 139	in Paradise alone	Ibid., p. 101.
p. 148	our sorry carnality	John Updike, "Imagining Things," *The New Yorker* (June 23, 1980): 96.
p. 148	what it "means"	Le Guin, personal letter, March 25, 1980.

Chapter 8

p. 152	said spontaneously, "Marriage"	Le Guin, *The Language of the Night:*, p. 143.
p. 153	repelled by science	Ibid., p. 26.
p. 153	form of fantasy	Ibid., p. 124.

The author acknowledges permission to quote extracts from the following works:

A. E. HOUSMAN: Extract from A SHROPSHIRE LAD (XII), to the Society of Authors as the literary representative of the Estate of A. E. Housman and Jonathan Cape Ltd., publishers of A. E. Housman's *Collected Poems*.

From "When I watch the living meet" from "A Shropshire Lad"—Authorized Edition—from *The Collected Poems of A. E. Housman*. Copyright 1939, 1940, © 1965 by Holt, Rinehart and Winston. Copyright © 1967, 1968 by Robert E. Symons. Reprinted by permission of Holt, Rinehart and Winston, Publishers.

LAO TSU, *Tao Te Ching*, transl. Gia-Fu Feng and Jane English. New York: Alfred A. Knopf, Inc., 1972. Copyright © 1972 by Gia-Fu

Bibliography

1. Works by Ursula K. Le Guin

A. Novels

Rocannon's World. New York: Ace Books, 1966.
Planet of Exile. New York: Ace Books, 1966.
City of Illusions. New York: Ace Books, 1967.
A Wizard of Earthsea. Berkeley, CA.: Parnassus Press, 1968.
The Left Hand of Darkness. New York: Ace Books, 1969.
The Tombs of Atuan. New York: Atheneum, 1971.
  Copyright © 1970, 1971 by Ursula K. Le Guin
The Lathe of Heaven. New York: Charles Scribner's Sons, 1971.
  Copyright © 1971 by Ursula K. Le Guin
The Farthest Shore. New York: Atheneum, 1972.
  Text copyright © 1971 by Ursula K. Le Guin
The Dispossessed: An Ambiguous Utopia. New York: Harper & Row, 1974.
The Word for World Is Forest. New York: Berkley Publishing Corp., 1976.
Very Far Away from Anywhere Else. New York: Atheneum, 1976.
The Water Is Wide. Portland, Ore.: Pendragon Press, 1976.
  Copyright © 1976 by Ursula K. Le Guin
The Eye of the Heron, in Virginia Kidd, ed., *Millennial Women.* New York: Delacorte Press, 1978.
  Copyright © 1978 by Ursula K. Le Guin
Leese Webster. New York: Atheneum, 1979.
Malafrena. New York: Berkley Publishing Corp., 1979.
The Beginning Place. New York: Harper & Row, 1980.

B. Essays, stories, and collections

"The Word for World Is Forest," in Harlan Ellison, ed., *Again, Dangerous Visions,* vol. 1. New York: Doubleday, 1972.

From Elfland to Poughkeepsie, introd. by Vonda N. McIntyre. Portland, Ore.: Pendragon Press, 1973.
"The Author of The Acacia Seeds and Other Extracts from the *Journal of the Association of Therolinguistics,*" in Terry Carr, ed., *Fellowship of the Stars.* New York: Simon & Schuster, 1974.
"Intracom," in George Hay, ed., *Stopwatch.* London: New English Library, 1974.
"Schrödinger's Cat," in Terry Carr, ed., *Universe 5.* New York: Random House, 1974.
Wild Angels. Santa Barbara, Ca.: Capra Press, 1975.
"Mazes," in Roger Elwood and Robert Silverberg, eds., *Epoch.* New York: Berkley Publishing Corp., 1975.
"The New Atlantis," in Robert Silverberg, ed., *The New Atlantis and Other Novellas of Science Fiction* by Gene Wolfe, Ursula K. Le Guin, James Tiptree, Jr. New York: Hawthorn Books, 1975.
Dreams Must Explain Themselves. New York: Algol Press, 1975.
The Wind's Twelve Quarters. New York: Harper & Row, 1975.
"The Diary of the Rose," in Jack Dann and Gardner Dozois, eds., *Future Power.* New York: Random House, 1976.
"The Eye Altering," in Lee Harding, ed., *The Altered I.* Carlton, Australia: Norstrilia Press, 1976.
"No Use to Talk to Me," in Lee Harding, ed., *The Altered I.* Carlton, Australia: Norstrilia Press, 1976.
"Solomon Leviathan's Nine Hundred and Thirty-First Trip Around the World," in Kaye Webb and Treld Bicknell, eds., *Puffin's Pleasure.* Harmondsworth, Middlesex, Eng.: Puffin, 1976.
Orsinian Tales. New York: Harper & Row, 1976.
"Gwilan's Harp," *Redbook* 149, 1 (May 1977).
"The First Report of the Shipwrecked Foreigner to the Kadanh of Derb," *Antaeus* 29 (Spring 1978).
"The Eye of the Heron," in Virginia Kidd, ed., *Millennial Women.* New York: Delacorte Press, 1978.
"SQ," in Alice Laurance, ed., *Cassandra Rising.* Garden City, N.Y.: Doubleday, 1978.
The Language of the Night: Essays on Fantasy and Science Fiction, ed. with introds. by Susan Wood. New York: G. P. Putnam's Sons, 1979.

C. Selected articles and interviews
"Prophets and Mirrors: Science Fiction as a Way of Seeing," *The Living Light* (Fall 1970): 111–21.

"The Crab Nebula, the Paramecium and Tolstoy," *Riverside Quarterly* 5 (Feb. 1972): 89–96.

"Science Fiction and the Future of Anarchy," with Charles Bigelow and J. McMahon, *Oregon Times* (Dec. 1974): 24–29.

"Vertex Interviews Ursula K. Le Guin," with Gene Van Troyer, *Vertex* 2 (Dec. 1974).

"Ursula K. Le Guin Interview: Tricks, Anthropology Create New Worlds," with Barry Barth, *Portland Scribe* 4 (May 17–23, 1975): 8–9.

"Ketterer on *The Left Hand of Darkness*," *Science-Fiction Studies* 2 (July 1975): 137–39.

"A Response to the Le Guin Issue," *Science-Fiction Studies* 3 (March 1976): 43–46.

"Ursula K. Le Guin: An Interview," with Paul Walker, *Luna Monthly* 63 (March 1976): 1–7.

"The Space Crone," *The Co-Evolution Quarterly* 10 (Summer 1976): 108–11.

Introduction, in Lee Harding, ed., *The Altered I*. Carlton, Australia: Norstrilia Press, 1976.

"Creating Realistic Utopias: 'The Obvious Trouble with Anarchism Is Neighbours,'" with Win McCormak and Anne Mendel, *Seven Days* (April 11, 1977): 38–40.

"*The Lathe of Heaven*," *Horizon* (Jan. 1980): 33–36.

2. Works edited by Le Guin

Nebula Award Stories Eleven. New York: Harper & Row, 1977.

Interfaces. (with Virginia Kidd), New York: Ace Books, 1980.

3. Works wholly or partly on Le Guin

Annas, Pamela J., "New Worlds, New Words: Androgyny in Feminist Science Fiction," *Science-Fiction Studies* 5, 2 (July 1978): 143–56.

Douglas Barbour, "*The Lathe of Heaven*: Taoist Dream," *Algol*, no. 21 (Nov. 1973): 22–24.

————, "Wholeness and Balance: An Addendum," *Science-Fiction Studies* 2, 3 (Nov. 1975): 248–49.

————, "Wholeness and Balance in the Hainish Novels of Ursula K. Le Guin," *Science-Fiction Studies* 1, 3 (Spring 1974): 164–73.

Neil Barron, *Anatomy of Wonder: Science Fiction*. New York and London: R. R. Bowker Company, 1976.

Martin Bickman, "Le Guin's *The Left Hand of Darkness*: Form and Content," *Science-Fiction Studies* 4, 1 (March 1977): 42–47.

Judah Bierman, "Ambiguity in Utopia: *The Dispossessed*," *Science-Fiction Studies* 2, 3 (Nov. 1975): 249–55.

Eleanor Cameron, "High Fantasy: *A Wizard of Earthsea*," *The Horn Book Magazine* 47 (April 1971): 129–38.

Elizabeth Cummins Cogell, "Setting as Analogue to Characterization in Ursula Le Guin," *Extrapolation* 18, no. 2 (1977): 131–41.

Joe De Bolt, ed., *Ursula K. Le Guin: Voyager to Inner Lands and to Outer Space*, with an intro. by Barry N. Malzberg. Port Washington, N.Y., London: Kennikat Press and National University Publications, 1979.

Samuel R. Delany, "To Read *The Dispossessed*," in *The Jewel-Hinged Jaw: Notes of the Language of Science Fiction*. New York: Berkley Publishing Corp., 1977.

Robert Galbreath, "Holism, Openness and the Other: Le Guin's Use of the Occult," *Science-Fiction Studies* 7, 1 (March 1980): 36–48.

John Huntington, "Public and Private Imperatives in Le Guin's Novels," *Science-Fiction Studies* 2, 3 (Nov. 1975): 237–43.

Fredric Jameson, "World Reduction in Le Guin: The Emergence of Utopian Narrative," *Science-Fiction Studies* 2, 3 (Nov. 1975): 221–30.

David Ketterer, "*The Left Hand of Darkness*: Ursula K. Le Guin's Archetypal 'Winter-Journey,'" in *New Worlds for Old: The Apocalyptic Imagination, Science Fiction and American Literature*. Bloomington: Indiana University Press, 1974.

Nadia Khouri, "The Dialectics of Power: Utopia in the Science Fiction of Le Guin, Jeury, and Piercy," *Science-Fiction Studies* 7, 1 (March 1980): 49–59.

Peter Nicholls, ed., *The Science Fiction Encyclopaedia*. Garden City, N.Y.: Doubleday, 1979.

Rafail Nudelman, "An Approach to the Structure of Le Guin's SF," *Science-Fiction Studies* 2, 3 (Nov. 1975): 210–20.

Joseph D. Olander and Martin Harry Greenberg, eds., *Ursula K. Le Guin*. New York: Taplinger Publishing Company, 1979.

Robert Plank, "Ursula K. Le Guin and the Decline of Romantic Love," *Science-Fiction Studies* 3, 1 (March 1976): 36–43.

David L. Porter, "The Politics of Le Guin's Opus," *Science-Fiction Studies* 2, 3 (Nov. 1975): 243–48.

Eric S. Rabkin, "Determinism, Free Will and Point of View in Le Guin's *The Left Hand of Darkness*," *Extrapolation* 20, 1 (Spring 1979): 5–19.

Thomas Remington, "A Touch of Difference, a Touch of Love: Theme in Three Stories by Ursula K. Le Guin," *Extrapolation* 18–19, 1 (Dec. 1976): 28–41.

Robert Scholes, "The Good Witch of the West," in *Structural Fabulation: An Essay on Fiction of the Future.* University of Notre Dame Ward-Phillips Lectures in English Language and Literature, vol. 7. Notre Dame and London: University of Notre Dame Press, 1975.

—— and Eric S. Rabkin, *Science Fiction: History, Science, Vision.* London: Oxford University Press, 1977.

T. A. Shippey, "The Magic Art and the Evolution of Words: Ursula Le Guin's Earthsea Trilogy," *Mosaic* 10, 2 (Winter 1977): 147–63.

George Edgar Slusser, *The Farthest Shores of Ursula K. Le Guin.* The Milford Series: Popular Writers of Today, vol. 3. San Bernardino, Ca.: The Borgo Press, 1976.

Darko Suvin, "Parables of De-Alienation: Le Guin's Widdershins Dance," *Science-Fiction Studies* 2, 3 (Nov. 1975): 265–74.

Donald F. Theall, "The Art of Social-Science Fiction: The Ambiguous Utopian Dialectic of Ursula K. Le Guin," *Science-Fiction Studies* 2, 3 (Nov. 1975): 256–64.

John Updike, "Imagining Things," *The New Yorker* (June 23, 1980): 94–97.

Victor Urbanowicz, "Personal and Political in *The Dispossessed*," *Science-Fiction Studies* 5, 2 (July 1978): 110–17.

Ian Watson, "The Forest as Metaphor for Mind: 'The Word for World Is Forest' and 'Vaster than Empires and More Slow,'" *Science-Fiction Studies* 2, 3 (Nov. 1975): 231–37.

——, "Le Guin's *Lathe of Heaven* and the Role of Dick: The False Reality as Mediator," *Science-Fiction Studies* 2, 1 (March 1975): 67–75.

George Woodcock, "The Equilibrations of Freedom: Pt. 2: Notes on the Novels of Ursula K. Le Guin," *Georgia Straight* 10 (Oct. 28–Nov. 4, 1976): 6–7.

4. Background material

Chuang Tzu, *The Complete Works of Chuang Tzu*, trans. Burton Watson. New York: Columbia University Press, 1968.

Padraic Colum, *The Children of Odin.* New York: Macmillan Company, 1920.

166 Ursula K. Le Guin

William C. Dement, *Some Must Watch While Some Must Sleep.* San Francisco: W. H. Freeman, 1972.

Edward John Moreton Drax Plunkett, Lord Dunsany, *A Dreamer's Tales.* London: G. Allen and Sons, 1910.

Harlan Ellison, ed., *Again, Dangerous Visions.* New York: Doubleday, 1972.

James George Frazer, *The Golden Bough: A Study in Magic and Religion.* Abridged ed. London: Macmillan, 1963.

————, *Leaves from The Golden Bough,* culled by Lady Frazer. New York: Macmillan, 1924.

Emma Goldman, *Living My Life.* New York: A. A. Knopf, 1931.

Paul Goodman, *Growing Up Absurd: Problems of Youth in the Organized System.* New York: Random House, 1960.

J. A. Hadfield, *Dreams and Nightmares.* Harmondsworth, Middlesex, Eng.: Penguin Books, 1954.

A. E. Housman, *The Complete Poems of A. E. Housman.* New York: Holt, Rinehart and Winston, 1965.

The I Ching or Book of Changes, the Richard Wilhelm translation rendered into English by Cary F. Baynes; foreword by C. G. Jung; preface to the third edition by Hellmut Wilhelm. 3d ed. Bollingen Series XIX. Princeton, N.J.: Princeton University Press, 1967.

Jolande Jacobi, *The Psychology of C. G. Jung.* New Haven: Yale University Press, 1962.

William James, *Essays on Faith and Morals,* selected by Ralph Barton Perry. New York: The World Publishing Company, 1962.

Carl Gustav Jung, *The Collected Works of C. G. Jung,* trans. R. F. C. Hull. London: Routledge and Kegan Paul: vol. 8, *The Structure and Dynamics of the Psyche* (1960); vol. 11, *Psychology and Religion: West and East* (1958).

Theodora K. Kroeber, *Alfred Kroeber: A Personal Configuration.* Berkeley: University of California Press, 1970.

————, *Ishi in Two Worlds: A Biography of the Last Wild Indian in North America.* Berkeley: University of California Press, 1961.

Petr Alekseevich Kropotkin, *Mutual Aid, a Factor of Evolution.* With foreword by Ashley Montagu and "The Struggle for Existence" by Thomas H. Huxley. Boston: Extending Horizon Books, 1955.

Lao Tsu, *Tao Te Ching.* Transl. by Gia-Fu Feng and Jane English. New York: Alfred A. Knopf, Inc., 1972.

Thomas More, *Utopia.* Trans. with an introd. by Paul Turner. Harmondsworth, Middlesex, Eng.: Penguin Books, 1965.

William Morris, *Stories in Prose, Stories in Verse, Shorter Poems, Lectures and Essays*, ed. G. D. H. Cole. London: The Nonesuch Press, 1948.

Joseph Needham, *Science and Civilization in China*. Cambridge, England: At The University Press, 1954–   , vol. 2, *History of Scientific Thought* (1956).

Rainer Maria Rilke, *Duino Elegies*, with English translations by C. F. MacIntyre. Berkeley: University of California Press, 1965.

Charles T. Tart, ed., *Altered States of Consciousness*. New York: John Wiley and Sons, 1969.

Holmes Welch, *Taoism: The Parting of the Way*, rev. ed. Boston: Beacon Press, 1965.

George Woodcock, *Anarchism: A History of Libertarian Ideas and Movements*. New York: The World Publishing Company, 1962.

Index

Adler, Alfred, 90
Again, Dangerous Visions, 2, 9, 99
Agnar (character), 19
Ainsetain (character), 106
Akaren (character), 59
Aladdin and the lamp, 87
*Alfred Kroeber: A Personal
    Configuration*, 2
Alice (character), 137
Allia (character), 147
"Alpha Ralpha Boulevard," 8
Altered States of Consciousness
    (Tart), 100
Amazing, 8
Amazing Stories, 5
Ana Jest (character), 127
anarchism, 10, 102–3, 105
    political theory of, 116
    unity of action in, 12
Anarchism (Woodcock), 117
Anarres:
    education of Anarresti, 109
    planet of, 103–23
    population of, 112
Andersen, Hans Christian, 87
androgyne, the Platonic myth of,
    75–76
androgyny, 64–68
anima, concept of, 61
animism, 94
Anna (character), 142

ansible, the, 17, 20, 98, 104–5
"April in Paris," 134
Argaven XVII (character), 63, 67
Arha (character), 49–55
Arren (character), 57–61
Aslan (character), 84
Asgard, 16
Astounding, 5
atheism, 140
Athshe and Athsheans, 96–101
Atlantis, 126
Atro (character), 113
Augmentor, the, 86
"Aussiecon," 11
Austro-Hungarian Empire, 131
"Author of the Acacia Seeds and
    Other Extracts from the
    *Journal of the Association of
    Therolinguistics, The*", 129

Barbour, Douglas, 85
Barzyk, Frederick, 95
battle of light and darkness, 41
    theme of, 74–75, 80
Bedap (character), 121
Beethoven, Ludwig van, 7
    allusion to *Ninth Symphony*, 128
Beggarman (character), 110–11
Beginning Place, The, 11, 130,
    145–49
    new departure for Le Guin, 149

169